AMBIENT 2018

The Eighth International Conference on Ambient Computing, Applications, Services and Technologies

November 18 - 22, 2018

Athens, Greece

AMBIENT 2018 Editors

Kropf Johannes, AIT - Austrian Institute of Technology, Vienna, Austria

Lasse Berntzen, University College of Southeast Norway, Norway

Printed from e-media with permission by:

Curran Associates, Inc.
57 Morehouse Lane
Red Hook, NY 12571

Printed by Curran Associates, Inc. (2019)

International Academy, Research, and Industry Association (IARIA)
412 Derby Way
Wilmington, DE 19810

Phone: (408) 893-6407
Fax: (408) 527-6351

petre@iaria.org

Additional copies of this publication are available from:

Curran Associates, Inc.
57 Morehouse Lane
Red Hook, NY 12571 USA
Phone: 845-758-0400
Fax: 845-758-2633
Email: curran@proceedings.com
Web: www.proceedings.com

Table of Contents

AMBIENT 2018

Forward

The Eighth International Conference on Ambient Computing, Applications, Services and Technologies (AMBIENT 2018), held between November 18, 2018 and November 22, 2018 in Athens, Greece, continued a series of events devoted to a global view on ambient computing, services, applications, technologies and their integration.

On the way for a full digital society, ambient, sentient and ubiquitous paradigms lead the torch. There is a need for behavioral changes for users to understand, accept, handle, and feel helped within the surrounding digital environments. Ambient comes as a digital storm bringing new facets of computing, services and applications. Smart phones and sentient offices, wearable devices, domotics, and ambient interfaces are only a few of such personalized aspects. The advent of social and mobile networks along with context-driven tracking and localization paved the way for ambient assisted living, intelligent homes, social games, and telemedicine.

The conference had the following tracks:

- Ambient devices, applications and systems
- Ambient services, technology and platforms
- Ambient Environments for Assisted Living and Virtual Coaching
- User Friendly Interfaces

We take here the opportunity to warmly thank all the members of the AMBIENT 2018 technical program committee, as well as all the reviewers. The creation of such a high quality conference program would not have been possible without their involvement. We also kindly thank all the authors that dedicated much of their time and effort to contribute to AMBIENT 2018. We truly believe that, thanks to all these efforts, the final conference program consisted of top quality contributions.

We also gratefully thank the members of the AMBIENT 2018 organizing committee for their help in handling the logistics and for their work that made this professional meeting a success.

We hope that AMBIENT 2018 was a successful international forum for the exchange of ideas and results between academia and industry and to promote further progress in the field of ambient computing, applications, services and technologies. We also hope that Athens, Greece, provided a pleasant environment during the conference and everyone saved some time to enjoy the historic charm of the city.

AMBIENT 2018 Chairs

AMBIENT Steering Committee

Yuh-Jong Hu, National Chengchi University-Taipei, Taiwan (ROC)
Naoki Fukuta, Shizuoka University, Japan
Jerry Chun-Wei Lin, Harbin Institute of Technology, Shenzhen, China

Kenji Suzuki, Illinois Institute of Technology, USA
Oscar Tomico, Eindhoven University of Technology, the Netherlands | ELISAVA Escola Universitaria, Spain
Lawrence W.C. Wong, National University of Singapore, Singapore

AMBIENT Industry/Research Advisory Committee

Evangelos Pournaras, ETH Zurich, Switzerland
Johannes Kropf, AIT Austrian Institute of Technology GmbH, Austria
Daniel Biella, University of Duisburg-Essen, Germany
Carsten Röcker, Fraunhofer Application Center Industrial Automation (IOSB-INA), Germany
Marc-Philippe Huget, Polytech Annecy-Chambery-LISTIC | University of Savoie, France
Tomasz M. Rutkowski, Cogent Labs Inc., Japan

AMBIENT 2018
Committee

AMBIENT Steering Committee

Yuh-Jong Hu, National Chengchi University-Taipei, Taiwan (ROC)
Naoki Fukuta, Shizuoka University, Japan
Jerry Chun-Wei Lin, Harbin Institute of Technology, Shenzhen, China
Kenji Suzuki, Illinois Institute of Technology, USA
Oscar Tomico, Eindhoven University of Technology, the Netherlands | ELISAVA Escola Universitaria, Spain
Lawrence W.C. Wong, National University of Singapore, Singapore

AMBIENT Industry/Research Advisory Committee

Evangelos Pournaras, ETH Zurich, Switzerland
Johannes Kropf, AIT Austrian Institute of Technology GmbH, Austria
Daniel Biella, University of Duisburg-Essen, Germany
Carsten Röcker, Fraunhofer Application Center Industrial Automation (IOSB-INA), Germany
Marc-Philippe Huget, Polytech Annecy-Chambery-LISTIC | University of Savoie, France
Tomasz M. Rutkowski, Cogent Labs Inc., Japan

AMBIENT 2018 Technical Program Committee

Mohammed Alia, AL Zaytoonah University of Jordan, Jordan
Mehdi Ammi, University of Paris-Saclay | CNRS/LIMSI, France
Cesar Analide, Universidade do Minho, Portugal
Eric Armengaud, AVL LIST GMBH, Graz, Austria
Maxim Bakaev, Novosibirsk State Technical University, Russia
Maria João Barreira Rodrigues, Universidade da Madeira, Portugal
Rachid Beghdad, Bejaia University, Algeria
Daniel Biella, University of Duisburg-Essen, Germany
Lars Braubach, Complex Software Systems | Bremen City University, Germany
Philip Breedon, Nottingham Trent University, UK
Ramon F. Brena Pinero, Tecnológico de Monterrey, Mexico
Valerie Camps, Paul Sabatier University | IRIT, France
Juan Carlos Cano, University Politécnica de Valencia, Spain
Kelsey Carlson, Independent Consultant, USA
Carlos Carrascosa, Universidad Politécnica de Valencia, Spain
John-Jules Charles Meyer, Utrecht University, The Netherlands
DeJiu Chen, KTH Royal Institute of Technology, Sweden
Albert M. K. Cheng, University of Houston, USA
William Cheng Chung Chu, Tunghai University, Taiwan

Juan Manuel Corchado Rodríguez, University of Salamanca, Spain
Mauro Dragone, Heriot-Watt University | Edinburgh Center for Robotics, UK
Rachida Dssouli, Concordia University, Canada
Mauro Dragone, Heriot-Watt University | Edinburgh Center for Robotics, UK
Duarte Duque, 2Ai - Polytechnic Institute of Cávado and Ave, Barcelos, Portugal
Christiane Eichenberg, Sigmund Freud University Vienna, Austria
Ahmed El Oualkadi, Abdelmalek Essaadi University, Morocco
Larbi Esmahi, Athabasca University, Canada
Imad Ez-zazi, National School of Applied Sciences of Tangier | University of Abdelmalek Essaadi, Morocco
Biyi Fang, Michigan State University, USA
Gianni Fenu, University of Cagliari, Italy
Jesus Fontecha, University of Castilla-La Mancha, Spain
Naoki Fukuta, Shizuoka University, Japan
Claudio Gallicchio, Universita' di Pisa, Italy
Matjaz Gams, Jožef Stefan Institute - Ljubljana, Slovenia
Musab Ghadi, Lab-STICC | University of Bretagne Occidentale, France
Marie-Pierre Gleizes, IRIT, France
Huan Gui, University of Illinois at Urbana-Champaign, USA
Maki Habib, American University in Cairo, Egypt
Ileana Hamburg, Institut Arbeit und Technik, Germany
Ibrahim A. Hameed, Norwegian University of Science and Technology (NTNU) in Ålesund, Norway
Ahmad Harb, German Jordanian University, Jordan
Jean Hennebert, iCoSys Institute | University of Applied Sciences HES-SO, Fribourg, Switzerland
Mehrdad Hessar, University of Washington, USA
Tzung-Pei Hong, National University of Kaohsiung, Taiwan
Yining Hu, University of New South Wales / Data61-CSIRO, Australia
Yuh-Jong Hu, National Chengchi University-Taipei, Taiwan (ROC)
Marc-Philippe Huget, Polytech Annecy-Chambery-LISTIC | University of Savoie, France
Reyes Juárez Ramírez, Universidad Autonoma de Baja California, Mexico
Martin Kampel, Vienna University of Technology, Austria
Viirj Kan, Primitive Labs / Samsung Research America, USA
Imrul Kayes, Sonobi, Inc., USA
Dina Khattab, Ain Shams University, Cairo, Egypt
Maher Khemakhem, King Abdulaziz University, Jeddah, KSA
Johannes Kropf, AIT Austrian Institute of Technology GmbH, Austria
Adam Krzyzak, Concordia University, Montreal, Canada
Markus Kucera, Ostbayerische Technische Hochschule Regensburg (OTH Regensburg), Germany
Frédéric Le Mouël, INSA Lyon, France
Fedor Lehocki, National Centre of Telemedicine Services | Slovak University of Technology, Slovakia
Lenka Lhotská, Czech Institute of Informatics, Robotics and Cybernetics | Czech Technical

University in Prague, Czech Republic
Jerry Chun-Wei Lin, Harbin Institute of Technology, Shenzhen, China
José Luís Silva, Instituto Universitário de Lisboa (ISCTE-IUL), ISTAR-IUL / M-ITI, Portugal
Irene Mavrommati, Hellenic Open University, Patras, Greece
Vittorio Miori, Institute of Information Science and Technologies "A. Faedo" (ISTI) | CNR - National Research Council of Italy, Pisa, Italy
El Houssaini Mohammed-Alamine, Chouaib Doukkali University, El Jadida, Morocco
Jouini Mouna, University of Tunis, Tunisia
Keith V. Nesbitt, University of Newcastle, Australia
Gerhard Nussbaum, Kompetenznetzwerk Informationstechnologie zur Förderung der Integration von Menschen mit Behinderungen (KI-I), Austria
Eva Oliveira, IPCA - School of Technology - DIGARC, Portugal
Pablo Pancardo, Juarez Autonomous University of Tabasco, Mexico
Ivan Pires, University of Beira Interior, Covilhã / Altran Portugal, Lisbon, Portugal
Evangelos Pournaras, ETH Zurich, Switzerland
Rafael Pous, Universitat Pompeu Fabra, Spain
Sigmundo Preissler Jr., Universidade do Contestado, Brazil,
Antonio M. Rinaldi, Università degli Studi di Napoli Federico II, Italy
Michele Risi, University of Salerno,Italy
Carsten Röcker, Fraunhofer Application Center Industrial Automation (IOSB-INA), Germany
Michele Ruta, Polytechnic University of Bari, Italy
Tomasz M. Rutkowski, Cogent Labs Inc., Japan
Khair Eddin Sabri, The University of Jordan, Jordan
Jose Ivan San Jose Vieco, University of Castilla-La Mancha, Spain
Peter Schneider-Kamp, University of Southern Denmark, Denmark
Floriano Scioscia, Polytechnic University of Bari, Italy
Riaz Ahmed Shaikh, King Abdulaziz University, Saudi Arabia
Jingbo Shang, University of Illinois, Urbana-Champaign, USA
Sheng Shen, University of Illinois at Urbana-Champaign, USA
Ingo Siegert, Otto von Guericke University Magdeburg, Germany
Carine Souveyet, Université Paris 1 Panthéon-Sorbonne, France
Andreas Stainer-Hochgatterer, AIT Austrian Institute of Technology GmbH, Austria
Mu-Chun Su, National Central University, Taiwan
Kenji Suzuki, Illinois Institute of Technology, USA
Oscar Tomico Plasencia, Eindhoven University of Technology, Netherlands
Alexandra Voit, University of Stuttgart, Germany
Yunsheng Wang, Kettering University, USA
Lawrence W.C. Wong, National University of Singapore, Singapore
Xiang Xiao, Google Inc., USA
Qiumin Xu, Google, USA
Kin-Choong Yow, Gwangju Institute of Science and Technology, South Korea
Chuan Yue, Colorado School of Mines, USA
Yang Zhang, Human-Computer Interaction Institute | Carnegie Mellon University, USA
Zixing Zhang, Universität Passau, Germany

Copyright Information

For your reference, this is the text governing the copyright release for material published by IARIA.

The copyright release is a transfer of publication rights, which allows IARIA and its partners to drive the dissemination of the published material. This allows IARIA to give articles increased visibility via distribution, inclusion in libraries, and arrangements for submission to indexes.

I, the undersigned, declare that the article is original, and that I represent the authors of this article in the copyright release matters. If this work has been done as work-for-hire, I have obtained all necessary clearances to execute a copyright release. I hereby irrevocably transfer exclusive copyright for this material to IARIA. I give IARIA permission or reproduce the work in any media format such as, but not limited to, print, digital, or electronic. I give IARIA permission to distribute the materials without restriction to any institutions or individuals. I give IARIA permission to submit the work for inclusion in article repositories as IARIA sees fit.

I, the undersigned, declare that to the best of my knowledge, the article is does not contain libelous or otherwise unlawful contents or invading the right of privacy or infringing on a proprietary right.

Following the copyright release, any circulated version of the article must bear the copyright notice and any header and footer information that IARIA applies to the published article.

IARIA grants royalty-free permission to the authors to disseminate the work, under the above provisions, for any academic, commercial, or industrial use. IARIA grants royalty-free permission to any individuals or institutions to make the article available electronically, online, or in print.

IARIA acknowledges that rights to any algorithm, process, procedure, apparatus, or articles of manufacture remain with the authors and their employers.

I, the undersigned, understand that IARIA will not be liable, in contract, tort (including, without limitation, negligence), pre-contract or other representations (other than fraudulent misrepresentations) or otherwise in connection with the publication of my work.

Exception to the above is made for work-for-hire performed while employed by the government. In that case, copyright to the material remains with the said government. The rightful owners (authors and government entity) grant unlimited and unrestricted permission to IARIA, IARIA's contractors, and IARIA's partners to further distribute the work.

A Rhetoric of Smart Carpet in the Age of Disruption

Leveraging IoT, Blockchain, and Platform for Value Co-Creation

Amirhossein Roshanzamir, Vishanth Weerakkody, Vignesh Yoganathan
Bradford University School of Management
Bradford, UK
Email:{A.H.Roshanzamir, V.Weerakkody, V.Yoganathan}@bradford.ac.uk

Abstract – **The luxury goods industry has experienced evolving consumer preferences, emerged from innovation and growth in the sharing economy and driven by digital technologies. On one side, the sharing economy has disrupted traditional luxury brands by providing or sharing access to goods and services through online platforms. On another side, the entire value chain of luxury goods, from procuring raw materials, design and production, delivery, product co-creation, up to customer service, in-store experience, and even consumption are transformed by digital technologies. The purpose of this study is to explore the role of digital technologies including the Internet of Things (IoT), blockchain and platform models, to disrupt the luxury industry. This paper suggests a novel and practical framework to transform handmade carpet to smart carpet and co-create value with potential customers in order to build trust and influence their buying behavior. The framework illustrates, for the first time, how the unmatched power of a brand story can be leveraged and authenticated by digital technologies and through active contribution of customers.**

Keywords–Smart Carpet; Luxury goods; The Sharing economy, Disruption; Digital technologies; Start-up; Brand Story; Co-creation; IoT; Blockchain; Platform models.

I. INTRODUCTION

Luxury products and services rely a great deal on brand intangibles and evoke a sense of myth and fascination. This is one of the reasons why the luxury sector grows faster than any other fields and thrives even during the challenging economic times. Considering all segments, the luxury market grew by 5% to an estimated €1.2 trillion globally in 2017, where sales of luxury cars continued to dominate the market by reaching €489 billion [1]. The value of worldwide personal luxury goods market —the "core of the core" is estimated to be €262 billion in 2017 with a heterogeneous group of 330 million individuals diversified by gender, cultural background, nationality, generation, attitude, and shopping behavior [1]. This huge market generated increasing interest in the luxury sector among both academics and practitioners [2][3] especially in the recent year with the advent of new trends and technologies.

On one side, the concept of sharing economy, which argues that the role of ownership is steadily being replaced by access, is gaining popularity and spreading among consumers, which ultimately redefines the luxury sector. The shift from " owning a luxury to just having access to it " is disrupting the luxury market and pushing brands beyond their traditional business models. The benefits of sharing platforms are lauded because of their possibilities to increase inter-personal interaction and provide more sustainable and environmentally friendly options in the market [4][5]. On another side, the widespread adoption of electronic commerce and online platforms transformed the value proposition of luxury brands from the product-centric of value creation to one that focuses on the personalized and overall experience of the process in which brands, consumers, and the respective networks co-create a superior value proposition through the entire supply chain. This is very challenging and threatening for traditional luxury brands since they are not equipped to provide the same sensory atmospheric conditions as the offline purchase [6]. Even, most luxury marketers questionably considered the Internet as a mass-market, which push them to substantial discounting and this ultimately discourages them to embrace digital and online business [7]. The sharing economy and digital technologies have huge implications for luxury brands and how they can be marketed and managed. The proliferation of online platform business models, blockchain, and the Internet of Things (IoT) have heralded a digital transformation to serve as a catalyst of growth and enable individuals to share goods and services and even contribute in design, production, and consumption of them. The platforms build up commercially ecosystems of suppliers and consumers in which enormous amounts of value can be created and exchanged [8]. Blockchain and IoT can embed tractability and visibility by recording every event and transaction within a supply chain on a distributed ledger [9] in order to integrate transparency, fair trade, and sustainability.

This paper, therefore, aims to explore the impact of digital technologies on transforming the luxury sector through value co-creation. By examining the smart carpet as a case study, this research argues that co-creating a brand story can be nurtured by digital technologies which ultimately builds trust and influences the purchaser's intentions and willingness to pay a premium for the product. The rest of this paper is organized as follows. Section 2 reviews the sharing economy and digital disruption in the luxury sector. Section 3 is focused on co-creation concept and evolving preferences of customers. In Section 4, the smart carpet is examined as a case study and a practical framework is suggested to illustrate how the power of brand story can be leveraged by IoT, blockchain and platform model in order to build trust and influence consumers' buying behavior. Section 5 analyzes the framework to examine how successful it can be in the global marketplace. The final section summarizes the contributions and suggests further domain for research.

II. THE SHARING ECONOMY AND DIGITAL DISRUPTION IN LUXURY SECTOR

Rogers [10] suggests that the world of marketing is shifting from mass market to customer networks in which the core behavior of customers is focused on access, connect, engage, customize and collaborate. Kotler [11] describes how marketing has evolved from product-driven marketing (1.0) to customer-centric marketing (2.0) to human-centric marketing (3.0) and now value-driven marketing (4.0). The term "value" has received lots of attention especially from scholars and practitioners in marketing discipline and in its simplest definition means price. If we take more professional approach value refers to the buyer's existing benefits over what he or she paid for. These benefits or values can be of three types ; functional value – the value of a product's features and functions, the economic value – what the product benefits are worth in terms of time and money and finally emotional value – the psychological benefits that they get from buying, using, and owning products [12]. The latter is very important within the luxury sector as luxury customers are placing more emphasis on the emotional value, such as closeness and involvement with brands when making their purchase decisions [13][14].

The consumer preferences of emotional value and involvement within the luxury sector are now influenced by the sharing economy and digital technologies. The concept of sharing economy argues that the role of ownership is steadily being replaced by access and companies and consumers are less likely to exchange goods and service in markets [15] within the new era. As such, a growing number of consumers are engaging in access-based consumption, where consumers gain access to the products they seek, but no transfer of ownership takes place [16]. In this scenario, suppliers lease, rent or charge subscription or membership fee, and consumers just pay for the temporary experience or short-term use of goods and services [15][17]. With the advancement of information technology and widespread use of social media [18][19] the sharing economy enables people to collaboratively make use of under-utilized inventory through fee-based sharing activities on online platforms [20]. Today's prominent online peer-to-peer platforms including Uber (owns no taxi), Airbnb (owns no property) and Alibaba (owns no stock) which are driven by social relations as well as prices, facilitate the use of underutilized labor and assets and disrupt their relevant industry. Disruption is associated in part with "Disruptive Innovation Theory" coined by Clayton Christensen [21] and refers to the fact that companies are disrupted because of their success, that they are so invested in a wonderfully profitable way to extract the most money from product, and doing it so well, they allow new entrants to offer an inferior product or service which is cheaper and more accessible. As such incumbents never seek to explore ways to do things differently and become vulnerable to a new technology at a lower price point which moves up market, eventually displacing established competitors [21].Williams [22] also argues that in some cases, threats to a company's business model come less from direct competitors than from high-impact innovation in a seemingly unrelated market. The new technologies often enter at the bottom of the market which is ignored by established companies and then new ventures grow and beat the old systems from that point [22]. The tremendous success of the world's largest taxi firm (Uber), the world's largest provider of accommodation (Airbnb) and the world's largest retailer (Alibaba) testifies that they did not come from competitors in the same industry or even from companies with a similar business model. Rather all of them emerged from the sharing economy platforms as start-ups and forged by digital technologies and ultimately disrupted their respective industry. In line with these success stories, it is assumed that owning lots of things is going to be outdated in a fast-paced luxury sector and most of the resources are borrowed or outsourced in a transition from ownership to the sharing economy. In "The Digital Transformation Playbook" Rogers argues that disruption happens when an existing industry faces a challenger that offers greater value to the customers in a way that existing firms cannot compete with directly [23]. The five domains of digital transformation" described by Rogers [23] builds a solid foundation to explain how digitalization is reshaping customers, competition, data, innovation, and value domains. Table I sets out strategic themes and key concepts as businesses move from the analog era to the digital age. The first and most important domain is the customers. Digital technologies have transformed the whole customer expectation and experience. In fact, luxury goods and services are now sought, sampled, and purchased in very different ways than before and consumers expect competent e-commerce, engaging and exciting interactions on social media, and multiple channels for interaction. [24]. The customers are now empowered with digital tools and require extremely personalized experience even by asking to shape the products and services. These requirements create a new ground of competition for the luxury brand and drive them toward building up an interactive platform to communicate with their customers.

TABLE I. THE FIVE DOMAINS OF DIGITAL TRANSFORMATIONS [23]

DOMAIN	STRATEGIC THEMES
Customers	Harness Customer Networks
Competition	Build Platforms, not just products
Data	Turn data into assets
Innovation	Innovate by rapid experimentation
Value	Adapt value proposition

Rogers [23] argues the value of a platform grows as more people use it and this due to the customer's expectation of bilateral value exchange. In fact, the platform can constantly improve its own features and increase participant benefits by creating a feedback loop. The data is an important asset which must be collected through online portals. Today, luxury brands can utilize social media and mobile apps for exploring customer's requirements, building communities of potential customers and using analytics and data mining to know them better and ultimately to offer personalized and customized services. Digitalization, as discussed by Rogers [23], provides a solid platform for a company to constantly experiment, test each of new ideas, measure customer response, and iterate on what it learns. Innovation is also leveraged through crowdsourcing and receiving feedbacks via social media and platforms. These are all invaluable for designing new products and services and improving the existing one as Parker [8] argues innovation is no longer the province of in-house experts and research and development labs. Lastly, digital technologies enable luxury brands to enhance, extend or reshape the customer value proposition with digital contents and engagement, i.e., to offer better, faster and customized products and services which resonates with their personal lifestyle [24].

While some luxury brands seek solutions to digitally automate their existing operations, we observe a few luxury start-ups are shaking up the industry [25] by aggregating many luxury e-commerce sites into a personalized feed and universal shopping cart [25][26] and extracting the most value from platform business model. The platform as discussed by Parker [8] offers reach, speed, convenience, and efficiency to customize the customer's requirements on luxury brand online shops. The possibility to capture data about customers' preferences and then develop and deliver the customized products in the quickest manner can be considered other benefits which are implemented by start-ups who focus on access rather than ownership. These new ventures aim to replace ownership with access where users can register on a platform and rent luxury items such as accessories and jewelry on a weekly or monthly basis. These start-ups work on everything from lab-grown diamonds to luxury subscription services to blockchain for authenticating luxury products. Some also launch new brands and/or help incumbents by offering them luxury-specific technology tools [27]. A good example is Rent the Runway [28] founded in 2009, an online platform which rents clothes and accessories for women with different plans. Eleven James [29] founded in 2013 is another online platform which provides access to a diverse collection of luxury watches for both men and women through subscription service. Dou Bao Bao and Y-Closet are two Chinese start-ups which provide access to a high-end designer handbag and a high-end clothing respectively by following rental business model [30]. Dou Bao Bao launched its platform on WeChat, and also released an official app and is now planning to expand the service to other Asian countries including Malaysia, Thailand, Vietnam, and Korea as the model far exceeded the company's expectations [30][31]. Y-Closet follows the rental business model and charges a monthly subscription fee of RMB 499 (USD$73) in which consumers have the option to select three cloths per month and swap them out as many times as they wish where delivery is included in the fee [30][31]. The next trend could be for the consumers to exchange each-others' items through the platforms. There are blockchain start-ups such as CEDEX [32] and BitCar [33] who focus on a single type of asset — diamonds and luxury cars, respectively. Switzerland-based Tend [34] is planning to offer a multitude of assets for investment purpose such as vineyards, watches and other luxury items. All three start-ups are still at very early-stage and planning to raise several millions of dollars through initial coin offerings in 2018. We can, however, see that they are all examples for rising of the sharing economy and platform business which are disrupting the value proposition of traditional luxury brands and creating emerging opportunities.

Acquiera et. al [35] conceptualize the sharing economy to rest on three foundational cores including Access economy, Platform economy, and Community-based economy. The sharing economy facilitates collaborative production and consumption and drives the concept of value co-creation [36].

III. VALUE CO-CREATION IN LUXURY BRANDS

Value co-creation, which refers to the practices a company uses to collaborate with its stakeholders during the design, development, and deployment of its products and services [37], is an emerging concept and was coined by Prahalad and Ramaswamy. It replaces the hierarchical approach to management and the linear approach to innovation by affording all stakeholders the possibility to influence and bring forth meaningful and relevant solutions in a collaborative environment from product design to product consumption [38]-[40]. Value co-creation has been triggered and driven by digital technologies in recent years [41]-[43]. These technologies can facilitate and transform the vast user-generated data and input into socially and economically valuable products and services [44]. In the era of big data, every change in customer behavior, location, or even physiological data can be recorded and analyzed [45]. In fact, big data allows firms to uncover unforeseen patterns about customers, businesses, and markets [15] while offering the firms opportunities to track customer behavior and measure outcomes of competitive strategies[16][17]. Modern luxury products usually commit to a brand story that includes a visionary myth and mission [46] and technology can expand this narrative to customers. Today, luxury brands should integrate their products with digital technology to add value and address "omnichannel interactions" including "integrated delivery service," comparable "promotions and rewards," and a "consistent brand image across all channels [47]. Although it is widely shown that user co-creation is beneficial in mainstream fashion [17], we must recall that the luxury sector has always distanced itself from consumers [48] in order to preserve the exclusivity and high status. Also, it is argued that luxury is art and should spring from designers' creative genius without that much input from the end user, therefore, user-designed luxury products are perceived to be lower in quality and fail to signal high status [49]. That is why to some extent consumers expect the artists to dictate what luxury should be and how it should be experienced [49][50]. As a result the luxury sector has implemented "a top-down, we-know-best-and-we-won't-listen-to-you attitude" [51]. In non-luxury categories, it is argued that "user design" i.e., drawing on users' ideas and designs for new products, will enable firms to achieve a number of positive benefits [52][53] including reducing new product development costs, improving time to market, and deriving innovative products which are better at meeting consumer needs and wants [17][20][53]. The Internet helps luxury brands increase consumer awareness and promote their images online by describing their brands' story and heritage[51]. However, Heine and Berghaus [54] argue that the majority of luxury brands still use mainly digital platforms to disseminate information to consumers in the classical sense of marketing rather than using social media to engage with their consumers. This strategy used to restrict the consumers' input to preserve since they walk the line between access and exclusivity, exposure and mystery, and restraint and expansion [46]. But now, the Internet is being utilized as a vehicle for luxury brands to enable consumers to share their personal experiences through narratives, co-creation and story-giving [54]. The direct interaction with consumers allows luxury brands turn storytelling into story-giving. As such these brands will not relinquish control of information creation while engaging with their consumers in the co-creation of their brand image. Tiffany & Co. [55] introduced the concept of the story giving as a powerful co-creation tool in their 2011 "What Makes Love True" (WMLT) which was a social media campaign with access to the e-commerce section of the company main website and studies shows that story-giving provide them with new opportunities to co-create stories about the brand while maintaining performance and paucity [55]. Schreier et al. [56] find that consumers evaluate a product more positively and indicate stronger purchase intentions if it is labeled as created by users instead of by the firm's internal designers. All these have created serious challenges as how to accommodate with the rise of co-creation trend which pushes luxury brands to shift their business model from a product-centric view of value creation to one that focuses on personalized and collaborative brand experiences.

IV. FRAMEWORK DEVELOPMENT AND CASE STUDY

Most successful start-ups like Uber and Airbnb have tried to improve people's life by solving something, empowering people, delivering value, fitting into their lives and giving people time back. However, many of them have challenges in building up their corporate brand at the initial stage as they had no resources, such as money and internal structure, nor did they have customers or even a consistent idea how the end-product should look like [57][58]. In fact, for a start-up, "visibility creates Opportunities", the faster it gets visible the closer the possibility of a business success is [59]. Moreover, the digital era has provided start-ups with tremendous opportunities to communicate and engage with their potential customers and stakeholders but substantial risks at the same time. Young ventures have specific branding needs due to their lack of resources [60], lack of internal structures and processes [60], and fundamental need to build a reputation [61] in order to find customers and investors. Venkatesh [62] identifies some of the challenges for start-up brand building including financial, legal and reputational risks, gaining traction and scaling-up. As such start-up branding cannot be addressed in a holistic approach since a new venture follows a growth curve where it goes through experimenting and testing its business model. Roshanzamir [57] suggests the EIC conceptual model in Figure 1 to break down brand building of a start-up into three stages and integrate it with start-up growth stages [57].

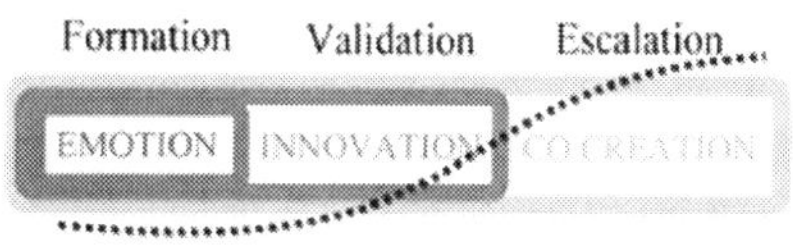

Figure 1. The EIC model for start-up branding in the digital era [57]

The EIC framework argues that the founders of start-ups must first have a strong sense of purpose, cause or belief to solve a market need or take advantage of an existing market opportunity and cultivate innovation and co-creation mindset. Second, they need to innovate things that make them special and differentiate them from their competition. Third, they must seek to jointly create and develop value as the tangible manifestation of the first two stages [57]. The authors propose a practical extension on the EIC model to illustrate how the power of a brand story can be leveraged by IoT, blockchain and platform models, in order to influence consumer buying behaviour. The concept of smart handmade carpet is, then, introduced and used as a case study here.

A. *Emotion*

For centuries, Persia has been famed as the major center of oriental carpet weaving and established the standards of architecture design miniature painting, and textile production. Carpet-weaving is considered to be one of the essential manifestations of Persian culture and art, and dates back to 500 B.C., during the Achaemenid according to evidence such as the 2500-year-old Pazyryk carpet. Though carpet weaving is now mechanized in many areas, the traditional handwoven carpet still has wide appeal throughout the world as a valuable masterpiece with a much higher price compared to machine made counterparts. The price of a handmade carpet is also determined by a number of factors including origin, size, design, age, purchase value, the materials as well as a brief history behind. Some traders document all these and issue a certificate of authenticity which can even be attested by international inspection companies. However, the authors argue that IoT, the blockchain and platform business can offer a game-changing solution and disrupt handmade carpet business by bringing transparency and trust to the supply chain, dealing with counterfeiting and increasing customer engagement. These technologies bring numerous possibilities to improve operations and contribute to a marketing campaign and build strong brands by generating an immutable digital certificate.

At the early stage of weaving a carpet, we can observe that the passion, skills, and talents of the designer and weavers are a bold contributor to producing a masterpiece. Innovation and Co-creation mindsets are other important ingredients for generating a brand story that must be cultivated from early days. In fact, a luxury strategy places a high priority on localized production to support the brand story and increase intrinsic value and the country of origin symbolizes expertise and cache [51]. That is why two pieces of carpet can be made of the same material within the same size, and even have a similar design, yet, Persian origin can reel the price by 5 to 10 times. By integrating IoT with blockchain, the smart carpet verifies the origin through smart tag embedded in the carpet from the time weaving started.

Chamrosh Technology [63] is a new start-up which is aimed to establish a platform in order to connect the luxury carpet weavers with the potential avid carpet fans and enthusiasms by leveraging digital technologies. The value proposition is to give the possibility of directly communicating with the weavers by reviewing the data and the full story of a carpet through digital tools i.e., video and pictures from the time weaving start. The platform utilizes IoT and blockchain to track the lifecycle of a carpet and validate the provenance such as origin and existing owner and other details in an immutable ledger which builds up the ingredient of a story. Griffin et. al. [64] indicates stories are often more important than hard facts because a brand or company's stories shape its reality. Walsh [65] argues storytelling is so critical to the brand building since stories are easy to remember and share, engage our feelings, shape our beliefs and enable us to see ourselves in a different light, and more importantly influence our behavior in accordance with these new perceptions, insights, and identities. The name of this start-up is smartly selected by the founders to generate a compelling story which gains buy-in from potential customers and guide, motivate and inspire stakeholders. Chamrosh is a bird in Persian mythology said to live on the summit of Mount Alborz and is sent by an angel to snatch invaders and drop them from mountaintops to protect the Persian Land [63]. The name generate a compelling story which is easy to remember, share and engage potential customers' feelings. Moreover, it is believed that integrating IoT, blockchain, and platform business model, indicated in Figure 2, would establish a structure to co-create value with potential customers in order to build trust and influence their buying behavior.

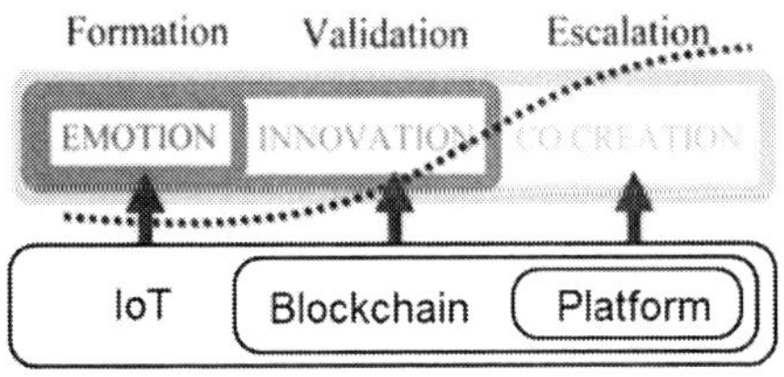

Figure 2. The practical extension of the EIC model

The framework breaks down the story of a carpet from the time procuring of knots and then weaving starts in a simple connection of cause and effect. The narrative of a carpet including the place and exact location of weaving, the name of weaver and designer together with video, audio and pictures are recorded, collected and shared with the potential customers as they are experiencing it as if it were their story. The customers feel what the weaver feels; they see what the weaver sees and experiences. Therefore, they memorize and retain chunks of information contained in the story since they watch the images and videos, hear the sounds, and feel the emotions which are recorded in a digital ledger that is distributed, decentralized, verifiable and irreversible.

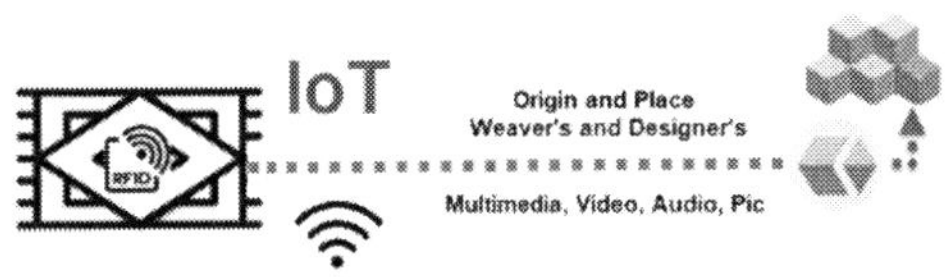

Figure 3. The rhetoric of carpet is recorded in the blockchain.

Figure 3 shows how the attractive rhetoric of a carpet can be leveraged in an immutable ledger on a vast network of computers and that put substantial monetary and emotional value at the heart of the weaving process.

B. *Innovation*

Innovation is considered to be a critical factor for long-term business success and organizations which have innovated successfully have typically been rewarded with growth, profits, and access to new markets throughout history, [66]. Though innovation can be the result of new technology; however, in some cases innovation is based on smart redeployment or combination of existing technologies. For example, iPhone as the most successful and amiable smartphone was not certainly the first one on the market either. Chamrosh is the first platform that fosters innovation in order to track a wealth of history behind the handmade carpet. It further builds a new experience and generates an authentic story for carpet buyers and art collectors by integrating digital technologies in the production, marketing and sales of handmade carpet in the world. The blockchain globally stores and collaboratively write a list of all transactions that have ever taken place within a given system [67] [68] and offers the possibility to keep the whole story of a carpet in a decentralized system. Therefore, when the owner of a smart carpet decides to sell his or her carpet, he or she could easily use the platform to create a digital certificate of authenticity and the next customer will be able to verify that carpet has not been stolen and that it was kept and maintained well. The uniqueness and novelty of this model are aimed to replace the legal norms and ownership rights of smart carpet without the need for a third-party authority to enforce exclusion rights. This is perfectly in line with recent arguments that the hybrid institution of property is a distributed ledger that can hold information about an intellectual property of right holders instead of a centralized government database [69] [70]. As the ownership records and other environmental data of the carpet are registered in real time system, all the pre and post owners of a single carpet, as well as the location of use, play a part in generating the story behind the carpet which can be verified. The process is described in Fig. 4 where the new ownership details will be added into the blockchain system together with some additional details including the temperature, humidity, and location of use. Here we see a paradigm shift in story-giving where the customer of a smart carpet can actively contribute in composing the story of it before selling the carpet to the next customer.

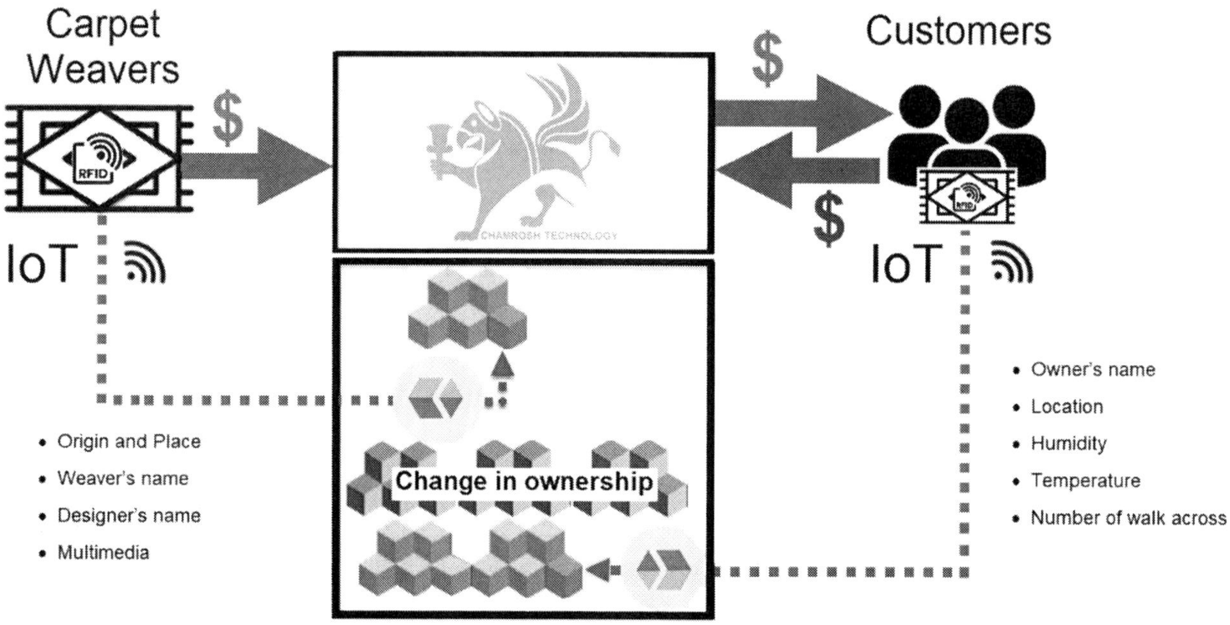

Figure 4. The smart carpet business model can address the trust issue by creating an authentic brand story [63]

C. *Co-creation*

Maxwell et. al [68] propose that blockchain technologies can become a new framework not only for the production (distribution and financing) of stories but also their generation. According to them the structural breaking down of stories into constituent parts and formulae is well established – from Aristotle's analysis of tragedy in Poetics to Georges Polti identifying 36 plots to Campbell's monomyth and Booker's seven themes. In the blockchain, each update or transaction like owner change is a new "block" added to the chain an encrypted manner without affecting the previous one. The implementation of property rights for physical objects through IoT and blockchain applications can eliminate some functions of third-party authorities for the enforcement of property rights [70]. Of course, it is still very early to conclude that some of the blockchain applications will be able to replace legal norms and property rights, yet, we can observe how some aspects of property relations in society are being replaced with the blockchain [71].

Co-creation practically happened in the third stage when a platform empowers different players including weavers, dealers, and buyers get together in order to produce a mutually valued output through a smart carpet which integrates digital technologies. Chamrosh utilizes the sense of trust and transparency embedded with the blockchain and IoT to generate a progressive story of a carpet from the time weaving starts. The smart tag or Radio Frequency Identification (RFID) chip will collect environmental parameters including temperature, moisture, number of time people walk across a carpet and more importantly the physical location through the radio signals without building a mechanical or optical contact. All these will be recorded in the form of a new block of the story across a peer-to-peer network as the carpet moves among multiple parties and owners.

The corporate story plays an important role in creating a position for the company against competitor [72] and could influence the impressions that audiences form of the organization and therefore build the corporate brand [73]. It has been argued that sharing consumers' positive stories about a brand can be a highly effective online marketing strategy [74]. In the smart carpet, we have a story anchored by the customer's lifestyle, driven by digital technologies and eager to provide extra verification on a carpet origin and lifecycle. Moreover, the novel integration of IoT, blockchain and platform, suggested here, addresses the question as to what extent corporate stories represent the reality of the organization raised by Spear and Roper [73] because the data about a smart carpet stored on the blockchain reflect the real events happen during ownership. Though they are not inherently accurate and mistakes can happen during recording time just as with a centralized database, however, integrating IoT and blockchain technologies can generate an authentic brand story that builds trust. In fact, IoT is the critical tool to disrupt the existing business paradigms of trading second-hand carpet with a new way of thinking, organizing, collaborating, and creating through decentralized applications. In these circumstances, a rhetoric of smart carpet in the age of disruption can engage the customer's feeling and influence their attitude and decision with the new perception and identify provided via digital technology. For example, those carpets which are placed at the holy sites of Islam and Christianity are traded at premium prices because the potential buyers assumed them to be blessed and cherished by the location of use. The smart carpet offers an innovative solution to trade these used carpets by ensuring the integrity of location and positively influence the purchase intentions and willingness of customers to pay a premium.

Moreover, the platform, accessible upon registration allows dealers and buyers to view and evaluate hundreds of carpets offered by different weavers and also former owners. The model also creates a pleasant experience and more choice for customers through aggregation of digital information by going beyond traditional factors such as age, design, and quality, promising them authenticity, trust, and transparency in an immutable ledger. Freemium model, which is built on an expectation of converting a portion of visitors to real buyers paying customers, increases the number of visitors to share views, comments, and feedback about each and every carpet. This will ultimately act as a strong marketing tool to promote the new start-up. Visitors can view and even verify the carpets but can neither buy nor sell within the platform. Only paid customers can utilize this advantage.

IBM Research has recently developed an Artificial Intelligent-powered counterfeit detector that verifies an item's authenticity using a smart phone's camera and then comparing the item to a database contained within a blockchain ledger [75]. The technology is accessible via a mobile app and can be used in Chamrosh to verify the authenticity of the carpet within a limited edition of carpets registered in the system.

V. DISCUSSION AND ANALYSIS

This section is dedicated to discussion and conducting performance analysis on smart carpet framework through the models offered by the most distinguished international leaders in the study of brands, branding, and marketing of the luxury goods.

First, Keller [76] argues that marketers have the opportunity to drive sales and build brands in ways never before possible by combining a diverse collection of new digital options added to the traditional media and communication options. He, therefore, suggests seven integrated marketing communications (IMC) choice criteria namely: coverage, cost, contribution, commonality, complementarity, cross-effects, and conformability [76]. These choices unlock the power of integrated marketing and can examine how effectively and efficiently they have been assembled. In order to evaluate the IMC choice criteria for smart carpet, we need to conduct a quantitative research which is beyond the objective of the existing paper. Nonetheless, we can review each criterion and examine how it resonates with the framework suggested by considering the luxury nature of smart carpet.

- Coverage for luxury brands needs to balance exclusivity with connection and honor and establish a soft barrier that makes a customer feel really special [46].
- Cost is the most important criteria to ensure an effective efficient communications campaign. It is assumed that innovation engraved in the product and platform business together with leveraging the power of social network would justify the cost.
- Contribution is certainly the most robust criteria and the essence of the smart carpet concept where the new avid carpet customer fan is encouraged to compose and be a part of a brand story through co- creation. This criteria also resonate with a concept of "Ueber-myth" a compelling story that gives the product meaning and reverberates emotionally with customer suggested by Schaefer and Kuehlwein [46].
- Commonality must ensure that information conveyed by different communication options shares meaning or elicits similar effects across communication options which is focused on co-creating value with potential customers and influence their attitude.
- Complementarity here is focused on covering the customer decision journey and desired positioning of smart carpet which can be met by integration of IoT and blockchain.
- Cross-effects offer creative synergy among the potential customers and leverage brand knowledge at a different stage of ownership. Since the new owner can review the ownership record and reality of former customers in the blockchain.
- Conformability is a bit tricky here since the whole concept of luxury is built on the product story weaves a tale of heritage and craftsmanship [46]. The enthusiasm of potential customers and their communication record can provide a glimpse into the heart and soul of the smart carpet.

Second, Joachimsthaler and Pfeiffer [77] claim companies need to understand consumers in the context of daily life experiences in order to leverage enormous opportunities for success. They propose Episodic Reconstruction Method (ERM) which attempts to broadly capture a wide range of situations and contexts of interests. Joachimsthaler [78] further insists that brand strategy must focus on the total transformative experience of consumers as people living, working and playing and then on linking emotional benefits to tangible proof and reasons in the superiority of the product. The value of our smart carpet model can be easily determined by the ERM framework. It allows the avid carpet fans to connect and engage with the smart carpet via latest technology and become part of the story. Rather than seeking to only improve the quality of carpet that is merely different from competitors' products, the smart carpet is focused on a brand story that creates desirability. The monetary value of the smart carpet increases through direct contribution of the new owner, the way he or she fits the carpet into his or her daily life, for example, the place it is located or the number of times the owner walk across it.

Third, the circles of luxury management practices developed by Nueno and Quelch [79] would offer more focused analysis. They [79] classify four distinct circles in managing luxury brands which can ensure the success in the global marketplace as design and communications management; product line management; customer service management; and channel management. Building on their model, we can see that Chamrosh business model perfectly fulfills these circles by harnessing digital technology to foster innovation and generate a favorable market acceptance. First, the nature of Persian carpet that only increases in value over time, is evolved from handmade carpet to smart carpet by harnessing technology and recording narratives in a digital ledger that is distributed and verifiable (communication management). Second, this evolution adds substantial monetary value every time the carpet is being bought and sold (product line management). Third, in Chamrosh platform each and every customer becomes expert in customer service, and relationship building by contributing in the rhetoric of carpet through generating a new block. In fact, the customer who buys a carpet today may purchase another item of much higher value from the platform or other customers tomorrow or even sell his or her carpet. Because more consumers are tempted to mix and match the narrative of carpets within the platform, the competition surges and cross-selling opportunities increase as they are seized (customer service management). Fourth, Chamrosh owns and is expected to manage the distribution channel by connecting weavers to customers and later customer to customer. As a developer of technology, the platform gets involved every time a carpet is bought and sold. It further charges a nominal fee to facilitate the transaction and generate a new block within the database (channel management). The other competitive advantage inherited within smart carpet platform is that it dedicates to the latest technology which is appealing to the young generation who are the potential customer of this technology in the coming years. As Nueno [80] argues, the future of many companies will depend to a great extent on teenagers' behavior and attitudes toward consumption which is shifting away from developed economies toward emerging markets, where the new wealth being generated is giving rise to an aspirational middle class. This young generation who are sometimes referred to as "Digital Millennials" or " Digital Natives" has many characteristics such as racial diversity, their status as the most educated generation to date, their low marriage and fertility rates but the most important one is that they are born with technology and considered heavy web users[81][82]. They currently form over a quarter of the American population, and about a quarter of the European Union's with an estimated purchasing power of $2.45 trillion worldwide [82]. Therefore, the challenge for smart carpet remains as for how to target this huge market.

Lastly, with the advent of Artificial Intelligence, we see some other applications of a smart carpet have such as physical therapy where the walking pattern of the owner is detected and analyzed and then with a help of therapist these patterns can predict mobility problems and correct them, have emerged, [83]. Also, the smart carpet can identify the presence of an intruder, acting as a kind of alarm system which detects environmental threats, like fires [83].

VI. CONCLUSION AND FUTURE RESEARCH

The sharing economy and digital technologies are disrupting the luxury sector by offering a new catalyst for growth and enabling individuals to share goods and services and even contribute in the design, production, and consumption of them. Blockchain and IoT can embed tractability and visibility by recording every event and transaction within a supply chain on a distributed ledger and then a platform provides an ecosystem of suppliers and consumers where enormous amounts of value can be created and exchanged.

This paper makes a few novel contributions to the domain of IoT, blockchain, and platform and their application in brand building, digital transformation in marketing of luxury products. It is the first study to suggest a framework for integrating IoT and blockchain and platform and apply the same in the marketing and branding field. Reviewing carpet weaving as one of the traditional businesses throughout the world and then utilizing the framework to transform this field from handmade carpet to smart carpet can be considered as the second significant contribution. Another key contribution is an emphasis on co-creating of a smart carpet brand by offering a paradigm shift in story-giving where the customer contributes to composing the story while handing over the ownership. Last but not least is that the framework addresses trust towards the smart carpet by creating an authentic brand story.

Future research is suggested to focus on conducting an empirical analysis especially on value elements and the value proposition of a smart carpet for different stakeholders in order to validate the effectiveness and credibility of the framework. The authors also believe that developing Minimum Viable Product (MVP) will help to conduct practical experience in order to humanized the new technologies, evaluate the pros and cons and bring them into daily life.

REFERENCES

[1] C. D'Arpizio, F. Levato, M. Kamel and J. Montgolfier, "Luxury Goods Worldwide Market Study," Fall–Winter 2017, December 22, 2017, https://www.bain.com/insights/luxury-goods-worldwide-market-study-fall-winter-2017/ 2018.09.20

[2] U. Okonkwo, "The luxury brand strategy challenge," Journal of Brand Management, Vol.16, No.5-6, pp. 287-289, 2009.

[3] K-P Hung, A.H. Chen, N. Peng, C. Hackley, R.A. Tiwsakul and C-L Chou, "Antecedents of luxury brand purchase intention," Journal of Product & Brand Management, Vol.20, No.6, pp. 457–467, 2011.

[4] J. Hamari, M. Sjöklint and A. Ukkonen, "The sharing economy: Why people participate in collaborative consumption," Journal of the Association for Information Science and Technology, Vol. 67, No.9, pp. 2047–2059, 2016.

[5] K. Hellwig, F. Morhart, F. Girardin and M. Hauser, "Exploring different types of sharing: A proposed segmentation of the market for sharing businesses," Psychology and Marketing, Vol.32, No.9, pp. 891–906, 2015.

[6] P. Arienti, "Global Powers of Luxury Goods 2018 Shaping the future of the luxury industry," EMEA Fashion & Luxury Leader. 2018; https://www2.deloitte.com/content/dam/Deloitte/at/Documents/consumer-business/deloitte-global-powers-of-luxury-goods-2018.pdf/ 2018.09.20

[7] U. Okonkwo, "Luxury Online Styles, Systems, Strategies," Palgrave Macmillan, 2010.

[8] G. G. Parker, M. W. Van Alstyne and S. P. Choudary, " Platform Revolution: How Networked Markets Are Transforming the Economy - and How to Make Them Work for You," W. W. Norton & Company, 2016.

[9] Z. Zheng, S. Xie, H.-N. Dai, and H. Wang, "Blockchain challenges and opportunities: A survey," International Journal of Web and Grid Services, 2017, pp. 1–23

[10] D. L. Rogers, "The Network Is Your Customer: Five Strategies to Thrive in a Digital Age," Yale University Press. Kindle Edition, 2011.

[11] P. Kotler, H. Kartajaya, and I. Setiawan, "Marketing 4.0: Moving from Traditional to Digital," Wiley. Kindle Edition, 2017.

[12] M. Sawhney, "Fundamentals of Customer Value," Kellogg School of Management, pp. 107–110 ; https://mthink.com/legacy/www.crmproject.com/content/pdf/CRM4_wp_sawhney.pdf / 2018.09.20

[13] C. D'Arprizio, C. Jilla, and M.A. Kamel, "The new rules of luxury," Bain & Company, Financial Times, 18 May, available at: https://www.bain.com/insights/the-new-rules-of-luxury/ 2018.09.20

[14] H.J. Choo, H. Moon, H. Kim and N. Yoon, "Luxury customer value," Journal of Fashion Marketing and Management: An International Journal, Vol.16, Iss.1, pp. 81-101, 2012.

[15] R. Clarke, " Big data, big risks," Journal Information Systems, Vol.26 Iss.1, pp. 77–90, 2016.

[16] S. Tirunillai, and G.J. Tellis, "Mining marketing meaning from online chatter: strategic brand analysis of big data using latent Dirichlet allocation," Journal of Marketing Research, Vol.51, Iss.4, pp. 463–479, 2014.

[17] C. Fuchs, E. Prandelli, M. Schreier and D.W. Dahl, "All That Is Users Might Not Be Gold: How Labeling Products as User Designed Backfires in the Context of Luxury Fashion Brands," Journal of Marketing: September, Vol.77, No.5, pp. 75-91, 2013.

[18] W.D. Hoyer, C. Rajesh, M. Dorotic, M. Krafft, and S.S. Singh, "Consumer Co-creation in New Product Development," Journal of Service Research, Vol.13, No. 3, pp. 283-296, 2010.

[19] S. Ogawa, and F.T. Piller," Reducing the Risks of New Product Development," Sloan Management Review, Vol.47 (Winter): p65-72, 2016.

[20] E. Von Hippel, "Democratizing Innovation: The Evolving Phenomenon of User Innovation," Journal für Betriebswirtschaft. Springer-Verlag, Cambridge. 2005

[21] C. M. Christensen, "The innovator's dilemma: When new technologies cause great firms to fail, " Harvard Business School Press. 2016

[22] L. Williams, "Disrupt: Think the Unthinkable to Spark Transformation in Your Business" Pearson FT Press; 2nd edition, 2015.

[23] D. L. Rogers, "The Digital Transformation Playbook: Rethink Your Business for the Digital Age," Columbia Business School Publishing, Columbia University Press. Kindle Edition, 2016.

[24] www.bcg.com/industries/consumer-products/luxury.aspx/ 2018.09.20

[25] https://www.cbinsights.com/research/future-luxury-trends/#subscription/ 2018.09.20

[26] https://apiumhub.com/tech-blog-barcelona/luxury-startups/ 2018.09.20

[27] P. Waelbroeck, "An Economic Analysis of Blockchains" CESifo Group Munich. pp. 1-28, 2018.

[28] www.renttherunway.com/ 2018.09.20

[29] https://elevenjames.com/about/ 2018.09.20

[30] https://jingdaily.com/luxury-rentals-china-sharing-economy/ 2018.09.20

[31] https://jingdaily.com/luxury-goods-rental-startups-explained/ 2018.09.20

[32] https://cedex.com/ 2018.09.20

[33] https://bitcar.io/ 2018.09.20

[34] https://www.tendswiss.com/ 2018.09.20

[35] A. Acquiera,T. Daudigeosb and J. Pinksec, "Promises and paradoxes of the sharing economy: An organizing framework" Technological Forecasting & Social Change Vol.125, pp. 1–10, 2017.

[36] T. Zhang, M. Farboudi Jahromi and M. Kizildag, " Value co-creation in a sharing economy: The end of price wars?" International Journal of Hospitality Management No.71, 2018.

[37] C.K. Prahalad and V. Ramaswamy, "Co-creating unique value with customers," Strategy & Leadership, Vol.32, Iss.3, pp. 4-9, 2004.

[38] C.K. Prahalad, "The co-creation of value," Journal of Marketing ; Vol.68, Iss.1, pp. 1-17, 2004.

[39] A. Payne, K. Storbacka., P. Frow, and S. Knox, "Co-creating brands: diagnosing and designing the relationship experience," Journal of Business Research, Vol.62, No.3, pp. 379–389, 2009.

[40] S. Lenka, V. Parida, D.R. Sjodin and J. Wincent, " Digitalization and Advanced Service Innovation: How Digitalization Capabilities Enable Companies to Co-Create Value with Customers, " Management of Innovation and Technology, No.3, pp. 2-5, 2016.

[41] S. Lenka, V. Parida and J. Wincent, "Digitalization Capabilities as Enablers of Value Co-Creation in Servitizing Firms," Psychology & Marketing, No.34, pp. 92-100, 2017.

[42] M. Holmlund, T. Strandvik and I. Lahteenmaki, "Digitalization Challenging Institutional Logics: Top Executive Sensemaking of Service Business Change," Journal of Service Theory and Practice, No.27, pp. 213-230, 2017.

[43] T. Brandsen, B. Verschuere and T. Steen, "Co-Production and Co-Creation" New York: Routledge, 2018.

[44] A.A. Efros, "Portraiture in the age of big data," Communications of the ACM, Vol.57 Iss.9, pp. 92-92, 2014.

[45] L. Yang, S. Madnick, R. Wang, F. Wang and Z. Hongyun, "A Cubic Framework for the Chief data Officer: succeeding in a world of big data," MIS Quarterly Executive, Vo.13, Iss.1, pp. 1–13. 2014

[46] W. Schaefer and J.P. Kuehlwein, "Rethinking Prestige Branding Secrets of the Ueber-Brands," Kogan Page, 2015.

[47] O. Abtan, C. Barton, F. Bonelli, H. Gurzki, A. Mei-Pochtler, N. Pianon and Miki Tsusaka, "Digital or Die The Choice for Luxury Brands," Boston Consulting Group, 2016.

[48] J.N. Kapferer and V. Bastien, "The Luxury Strategy: Break the Rules of Marketing to Build Luxury Brands," Kogan Page: London, UK, 2009.

[49] W. Ozuem and Y. Azemi, "Digital Marketing Strategies for Fashion and Luxury Brands," IGI Global; 1st edition, 2017.

[50] J.N. Kapferer, "The future of luxury: Challenges and opportunities," The Journal of Brand Management. Vol.21, Iss.9, pp. 716–726, 2014.

[51] J. N. Kapferer, "Kapferer on Luxury How Luxury Brands Can Grow Yet Remain Rare," Kogan Page. 2015.

[52] E. Colyer "Luxury Brands Confront Web 2.0," www.brandchannel.com, August 27. 2007

[53] D. W. Dahl, C. Fuchs, & M. Schreier, "Why and When Consumers Prefer Products of User-Driven Firms: A Social Identification Account" Management Science, Vol.61, No.8, pp. 1978-1988, 2015.

[54] K. Heine and B. Berghaus, "Luxury goes digital: how to tackle the digital luxury brand–consumer touchpoints," Journal of Global Fashion Marketing, Special Issue: Social Media Marketing and Luxury Brands, Vol.5 No.3, pp. 223-234, 2014.

[55] http://www.tiffany.com/ 2018.09.20

[56] M. Schreier, C. Fuchs and D. Dahl, "The innovation effect of user design: Exploring consumers' innovation perceptions of firms selling products designed by users" Journal of Marketing, No.76, pp. 18-32, 2012.

[57] A. Roshanzamir, " Dilemmas of Branding for Start-ups in Digital Era, " The Twelfth International Conference on Digital Society and eGovernments Rome, Italy, pp. 63-72, 2018.

[58] M. Nair "Why Is Branding Crucial For Start-ups ?" https://www.entrepreneur.com/article/279331/ 2018.09.20

[59] T. Abimbola, and C. Vallaster, "Brand, organizational identity and reputation in SMEs: an overview, " Qualitative Market Research: An International Journal, Vol.10, Iss.4, pp. 341-348, 2007.

[60] V. Rode and C. Vallaster, "Corporate branding for start-ups: the crucial role of entrepreneurs, "Corporate Reputation Review, Vol.8 No.2, pp. 121-135, 2005.

[61] A. P. Petkova, and V. P. Rindova, and A.K. Gupta, "How can new ventures build reputation? An exploratory study," Corporate Reputation Review, Vol.11, Iss.4, pp. 320–334, 2008.

[62] U. Venkatesh, "Branding Impetus for Start-Ups: Relevance and Rhetoric, " IGI Global, pp. 54-74, 2018.

[63] www.chamrosh.com/ 2018.09.20

[64] A.Griffin, M.B. Johnson, E. K. Fishman, K.M. Horton, P.T. Johnson, "The Power of Stories in Brands, Business, and Life," Journal of the American College of Radiology, Vol.14, Iss.4, pp. 573-574, 2017.

[65] B.C. Walsh, "The Power of Story: Bring Your Brand to Life," Nonprofit World, Vol.34, Iss. 4, pp. 18 19, 2016.

[66] J. Bessant and J. Tidd, "Innovation and Entrepreneurship" John Wiley & Sons. 2007

[67] D. Maxwell, "Story Blocks: Reimagining narrative through the blockchain" Convergence: The International Journal of Research into New Media Technologies Vol.23, Iss.1, 2017.

[68] D. Maxwell, C. Speed and L. Pschetz " Story Blocks: Reimagining narrative through the blockchain," The International Journal of Research into New Media Technologies, Vol.23, Iss.1, pp. 79-97. 2017.

[69] A. Ha, " Blockai Uses the Blockchain to Help Artists Protect Their Intellectual Property," 2016; . Retrieved from https://techcrunch.com/2016/03/14/blockai-launch/ 2018.09.20

[70] P. Brody and V. Pureswaran, "Device democracy: Saving the future of the Internet of things" IBM, 2014.

[71] G. Ishmaev, "Blockchain Technology as an Institution of Property", Metaphilosophy, Vol. 48, No.5, pp. 666-686, 2017.

[72] S. Roper and C. Fill, "Corporate Reputation, Brand and Communication," Pearson, Harlow, 2012.

[73] S. Spear and S. Roper, "Using corporate stories to build the corporate brand: an impression management perspective," Journal of Product & Brand Management Vol. 22, Iss.7, pp. 491–501, 2013.

[74] R.R. Gosline, J. Lee and G.Urban, "The power of consumer stories in digital marketing," MIT Sloan Management Review, Vol. 58, Iss.4, pp. 9-13, 2017.

[75] https://thenextweb.com/artificial-intelligence/2018/05/23/ibm-combines-ai-and-blockchain-to-turn-your-phone-into-a-counterfeit-detector/ 2018.09.20

[76] K.L. Keller, "Unlocking the Power of Integrated Marketing Communications: How Integrated Is Your IMC Program?," Journal of Advertising, Vol. 45, Iss.3, pp 286-301, 2016.

[77] E. Joachimsthaler and M. Pfeiffer, " Decoding Demand Opportunity, " Business Strategy Review, Vol. 21, Iss.1, 2010.

[78] E. Joachimsthaler, " Hidden in Plain Sight: How to Find and Execute Your Company's Next Big Growth Strategy," Harvard Business Review Press, 2017.

[79] J. L. Nueno and J. A. Quelch, " The Mass Marketing of Luxury" Business Horizons, Business Horizons, Vol.41, Iss.6, pp. 61-68, 1998.

[80] J. L. Nueno, " Teens Today, Young Adults in 2020 " IESE Insight , First Quarter, Iss.8, pp. 50-58, 2011.

[81] M. Serazio, "Selling (Digital) Millennials The Social Construction and Technological Bias of a Consumer Generation" Television & New Media, Vol. 6, Iss.7, pp. 599-615, 2013.

[82] K. Moran, "Millennials as Digital Natives: Myths and Realities" January 3, 2016 ; https://www.nngroup.com/articles/millennials-digital-natives/ 2018.09.20

[83] D. Zax "A Smart Carpet to Detect Intruders" https://www.technologyreview.com/s/429130/a-smart-carpet-to-detect-intruders/ 2018.09.20

Daily Life Monitoring System with Behavior Pattern Recognition Using Ambient Sensors

Hirokazu Madokoro, Nobuhiro Shimoi, and Kazuhito Sato

Department of Intelligent Mechatronics
Faculty of Systems Science and Technology
Akita Prefectural University
Yurihonjo City, Akita, Japan
Email: {madokoro, shimoi, ksato}@akita-pu.ac.jp

***Abstract*—This paper presents a novel life monitoring system using a home agent and ambient sensors as invisible sensors that fit living circumstances with consideration of privacy and Quality of Life (QoL) for achieving autonomous monitoring in daily life. The home agent has a key tag sensor, a human detection sensor, and a remote control sensor for detecting the states of a subject, such as going out (Out) or being at home (Home). The ambient sensors consist of a pad sensor installed in a bed sheet, a triaxial accelerometer inserted in a pillow, a human detection sensor installed near an entrance door, and a piezoelectric sensor installed near a refrigerator. The state of Home or sleeping on a bed (Sleep) is detected using ambient sensors that measure living behavior patterns in real time. As a preliminary experiment aimed at monitoring various life patterns of elderly people, we conducted a monitoring experiment during two months for four university students subjects in their 20s. For this system, sensor signals were stored in a server via a wireless router for visualization on a monitoring computer terminal in real time. We developed a method of recognizing three major life patterns (Out, Home, and Sleep) using machine learning which uses eight algorithms. To evaluate of recognition accuracy, we collected handwritten daily records from the respective subjects used for correct behavior datasets as ground truth. Experimentally obtained results revealed that the mean recognition accuracy was 83.61% for the first half of the monitoring experiment during one month with one-minute downsampled signal intervals. In the last half of the monitoring experiment, data acquisition was interrupted because of a failure of the home agent. We continued the evaluation experiment of life patterns with two delimited periods, which indicated recognition accuracies of 92.53% for 18 days and 93.85% for 27 days.**

Keywords–ambient sensors; home agent; life monitoring; quality of life; machine learning; random forest.

I. Introduction

Because of the rapid progress of aging societies and increased longevity worldwide, mutual support among generations has already reached its limit, as reflected in distortion of the population pyramids of many nations. The problems of increased numbers of single elderly people, nursing care among care receivers, rarefaction of regional ties, isolation, and marginalization are manifested not only in regional cities and country sides with high aging rates, but also in metropolitan areas with higher population concentrations. For monitoring elderly people from remote areas, the development of information and communication systems, supporting devices, and sensor systems is underway [1]. In particular, security measures to prevent elderly people from a solitary death is urgent in our current society [2].

Particularly, life-support and service robot platforms with communication and interactive functions, along with sensing and monitoring using unconstrained and invisible sensors have been unveiled, offering advanced functionality and performance [3]. These systems are able to monitor several subjects as care receivers in parallel; subjects are assumed to be in nursing facilities focusing on monitoring functions. Moreover, these systems can be used for 24 hours continuously if malfunction is avoided. The advantage of these systems is to send notifications containing information simultaneously and instantly to nurses, caregivers, and family members. These autonomous systems do not require so much as the push of a button or raising one's voice to collect active information.

For specialized sleep monitoring, sensor systems that send notifications with information related to bed leaving behaviors to care takers or nurses are already in practical use [4]. Moreover, robotic nursing care devices with a monitoring function used for elderly people who have Mild Cognitive Impairment (MCI) [5] have been developed. Evaluation methods and criteria have already been established [6]. Various criteria and specifications exist for monitoring sensor systems according to use cases and situations of use. The most important function is automatic and immediate notification of abnormal or unusual information related to care. Contingent circumstances occur if automatic notification is delayed.

As a novel approach to overcome these problems, monitoring systems that specifically examine life pattern rhythms in our daily life have been studied [7]. Actually, humans have individual life rhythms related to health, mind, and mentality. Particularly for elderly people, unsteady or confusing life rhythms cause bad effects of sleep deprivation related to health. Therefore, we infer that monitoring systems can detect the health conditions of elderly people immediately if life rhythms can be extracted using monitoring support systems.

This paper presents a novel life-pattern monitoring system using multiple hidden sensors for adaption to daily life with respect to privacy and Quality of Life (QoL). Our proposed system comprises a home agent and ambient sensors. The home agent has a key tag detection sensor, a motion sensor, and a remote controller detection sensor for recognition of a monitored person as home or out. The ambient sensor comprises pad-shape sensors installed in a bed sheet, a triaxial accelerometer installed in a pillow, a motion sensor installed near a door, and piezoelectric film sensor installed in a refrigerator. The ambient sensor measures life behavior patterns at home to determine normal home behavior or sleeping in a bed. Monitored signals are saved on a server using network storage via a wireless router with a visualizing function of signal outputs in real time from respective sensors. As a preliminary experiment before monitoring diverse life patterns of elderly people, we conducted a monitoring experiment for two months to observe four university students subjects. Moreover, we attempted to recognize life patterns from collected datasets using machine learning algorithms. This report presents details of related studies, our proposed system, and recognition results.

The rest of the paper is structured as follows. In Section II, related studies are presented, especially for smart sensors and daily life monitoring systems. Sections III and IV present our proposed method and experimental results obtained using our original datasets, respectively. Finally, Section V concludes and highlights future work.

II. Related Studies

Various methods and experimentally obtained results of daily life monitoring have been reported in earlier studies. From results of a recent study report, Morishita et al. [8] described a monitoring system that detected opening or closing of a door using a magnet sensor with a function to report the safety of a resident and an application to display sensor detection results. Although they conducted a practical test at a residence for low-income elderly people, monitoring results reflected merely movements between rooms through doors. Jiang et al. [9] proposed a monitoring system for use in nursing care facilities. They obtained original datasets related to daily habits in terms of eating and exercise using a dual-band Radio Frequency IDentifier (RFID) and virtual routing locational algorithms. They revealed that their proposed system, which included hush functions and certification protocols, provided high security with real-time processing. Although they revealed that the total burden of waiting data calculation and communication was low, this result merely reflected results from a computer simulation.

Park et al. [10] proposed a framework of a healthcare monitoring system for elderly people using wearable sensors. Their knowledge-based method with self-learning algorithms collected sensor signals in real time while maintaining network security. Nevertheless, they only proposed a framework without conducting evaluation experiments or system implementation. Sumalan et al. [11] proposed a vital sign monitoring system in terms of heart rates, respiratory rates, and blood pressure for elderly people using wireless sensor networks. Although their design concept was set as cost effective for actualizing an application, their proposal remained a system structure without experimentally obtained results.

Ghayvat et al. [12] proposed a daily life monitoring system using electric current sensors, load sensors, and contact sensors. They developed an original model to discriminate between normal or abnormal status. Furthermore, they conducted an evaluation experiment at an elderly home and a nursing care facility. However, the results remained a single tendency of time-series visualization because their study was geared towards the development of communication circumstances for smart homes based on wireless networks and Internet of Things (IoT).

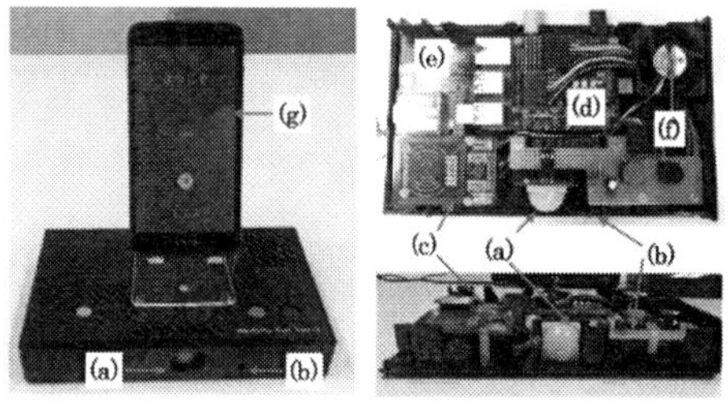

Figure 1. Home agent: (a) motion sensor, (b) remote controller sensor, (c) key sensor, (d) micro-controller board, (e) optional sensor board, (f) air cooling fan, and (g) smartphone

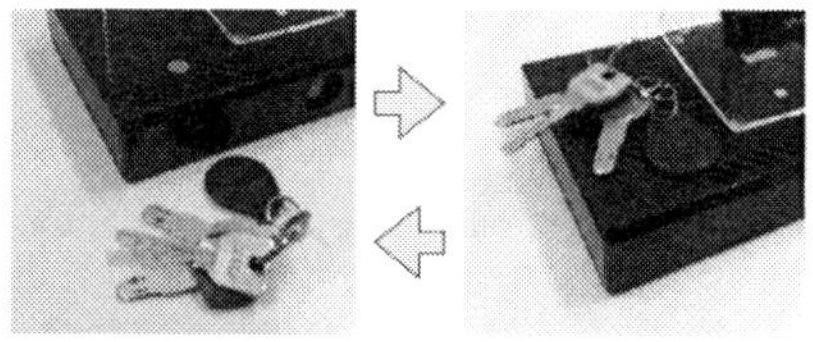

Figure 2. Key sensor. Card key type IC card is inserted into the blue key holder. The home agent detects the key using an RFID module.

Although they described details of the experimental setups, especially related to use at nursing care facilities, the experimentally obtained results were insufficient for a practical use.

As an example of research related to MCI, Mighali et al. [13] proposed a system of monitoring elderly behavior patterns. It incorporated wearable sensors and motion sensors installed in a home. The experimentally obtained results revealed that the mean recognition accuracy achieved 97% for 10 healthy subjects at a living circumstance in a general house. Nevertheless, the recognition targets were merely two patterns of static or dynamic states. Furthermore, the consideration of QoL was insufficient because the system used wearable sensors. Riboni et al. [14] proposed an ambient sensor system that was composed of wearable sensors and home sensors installed inside of electrical appliances. They conducted a practical test for the target of elderly people with MCI. However, the experimentally obtained results remained extraction of abnormal values without extracting patterns related to life rhythms. They merely reported discussion of a plan for the practical test without addressing details of experimentally obtained results.

Moreover, numerous international projects consisting of sensor networks and mobile robot prototypes have been conducted in terms of DOREMI (Decrease of cOgnitive decline, malnutRition and sedEntariness by elderly empowerment in lifestyle Management and social Inclusion) [15], RUBICON (for Robotic UBIquitous COgnitive Network) [16], and OPPORTUNITY (Activity and Context Recognition with Opportunistic Sensor Configurations) [17].

III. Proposed Method

A. *Proposed system structure*

Figure 1 depicts the home agent, named MaMoRu-kun [18]. The home agent is equipped with a key sensor, a motion

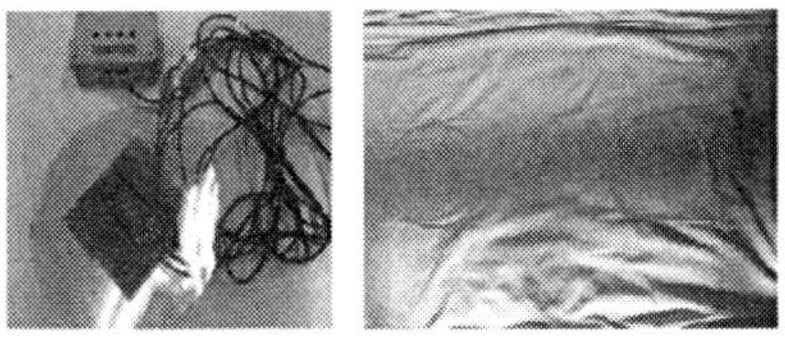

Figure 3. Bed sensor installed to the hip part with a sheet pocket. Piezoelectric films are used for this sensor.

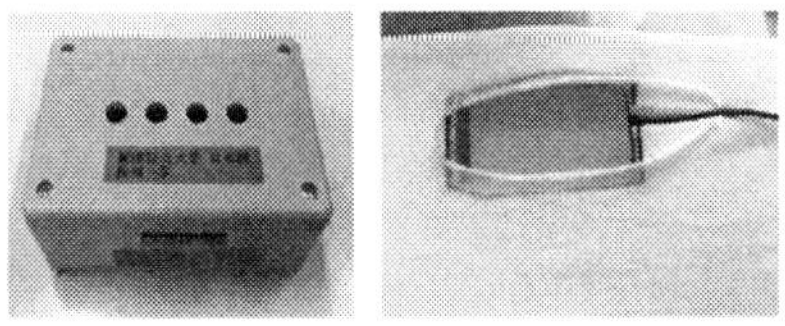

Figure 4. Pillow sensor. A built-in triaxial accelerometer is installed in a pillow with a wireless communication board.

sensor, and a remote control sensor. Figure 2 shows that the key sensor using a RFID-based wireless frequency Integrated Circuit (IC) card induction sensor (MFRC-522 RC522) detects the key status that was placed on the home agent. The motion sensor using a collecting electron type InfRared (IR) sensor module (SB612A) was installed to the front panel of the home agent. The remote control sensor using an IR module (SPS-440) was installed beside the motion sensor.

1) Home agent: We used a micro-controller board with Raspberry Pi 3 model B (BCM2837) as the main processing unit of the home agent. We implemented software to send the collected sensor signals to a router in a fixed interval using a wireless Local Area Network (LAN) of 802.11 b/g/n on a processing board. The board is equipped with an optional board (BME280) used for ambient sensors in terms of a temperature sensor, a humidity sensor, an atmospheric air sensor, and an illumination sensor. For this study, we did not use these sensors.

The sensor case is 120 mm wide, 199 mm long, and 35 mm high. Herein, the smartphone on the case top is used for a demonstration. Using a tethering function of the smartphone, the obtained sensor signals, which are collected with the home agent, can be sent to network storage. For this study, we sent sensor signals using a mobile wireless router.

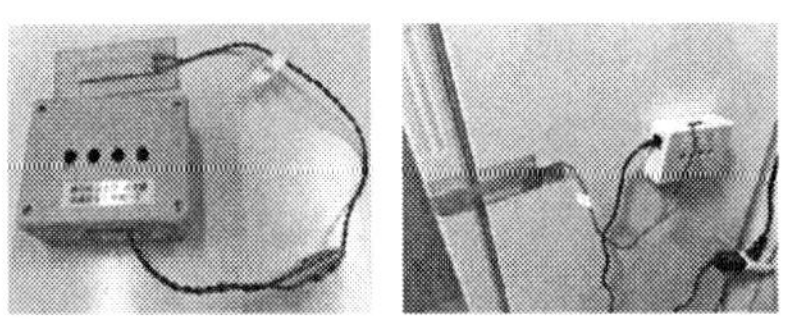

Figure 5. Refrigerator sensor. This is our originally developed sensor using a piezoelectric films bound with a urethane sheet.

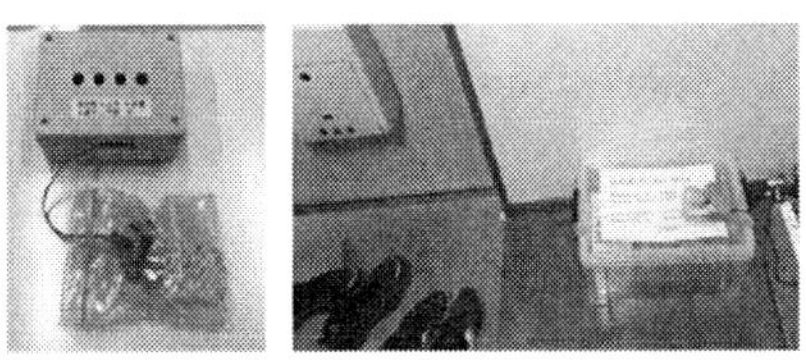

Figure 6. Motion sensor used near the entrance to detect a subject's arrival and departure.

2) Ambient sensors: Our proposed ambient sensor system comprises pad-shape sensors installed on a bed, a triaxial accelerometer installed in a pillow, a motion sensor installed near a door, and a piezoelectric sensor installed in the door of a refrigerator. Figure 3 depicts the bed sensor proposed in a report of our earlier study [19]. It was manufactured using a piezoelectric film based on our prototype sensor aimed at detecting bed leaving behavior. We used up to six sensors because the use is intended solely for detecting bed-leaving behaviors. For this study, we optimized the minimum structure for detecting the subject's status on a bed to recognize sleeping behavior patterns. As an optimized result, we used two channels after removing the detection of the body rolling over.

As hidden sensors, we installed bed sensors to the backside of the bed sheet. The sensor can be used not only with a bed, but also with a futon, a Japanese style bed, because of the installation on a sheet, which differs from existing sensors installed on the bed frame [20]. For this implementation, we sewed the sensor pads to a bed sheet near the hip part with a pocket for avoiding drift of the sensor position.

For a pillow sensor, we directly implemented a triaxial accelerometer (LIS3DSHTR) on a sensor board. Figure 4 depicts the pillow sensor and its implementation inside of a pillow after digging a hole from the backside. This sensor works as a transmitter to notify the system of urgent information of unusual body condition triggered by pillow movement. We proposed the basic design of the pillow sensor in our earlier study [19]. This is a revised model obtained after changing the size and wireless communication method from ZigBee to WI-FI. For the current implementation, an electric power cable is extended from the pillow to electric power supply. For dissemination, we will change it to a wireless power supply method.

Figure 5 depicts a refrigerator sensor: our originally developed sensor prototype was created by attaching a piezoelectric film to a door of the refrigerator. In our daily life, a refrigerator is frequently used as a home electrical appliance. Numerous models of refrigerators exist with diverse structures in terms of a freezer, a cold room, and a vegetable room. For this study, our measurement target is the door of a cold room, which has the highest frequency of opening or closing.

Figure 6 depicts a motion sensor: a similar sensor installed in the home agent, near an entrance door. For all sensor boards, we used a WI-FI module (ESP-WROOM-02) for a wireless connection as the assumption of IoT applications. Moreover, we installed them into a plastic case to avoid attachment on the bared board for purposes of durability because we used the sensor system for monitoring subjects at a home or other residence.

B. Method of recognizing life patterns

For this study, we attempted to recognize life patterns based on machine learning methods for monitoring signals obtained from sensors. Actually, deep learning, for which a framework was proposed by Hinton et al. [21], constructed a recognizer automatically based on unsupervised learning of repeated iterations using a huge dataset without annotation. Because of high generalization capability for unlearned datasets, deep learning has been applied widely to various fields, especially in computer vision problems. By contrast, plenty of calculation resources are necessary, especially for learning of large-scale neural networks with multiple layers, even more than ten layers.

As an enhanced combination, transfer learning [25] is used to reduce the burden of learning if recognition targets are generic objects [22], outdoor or indoor scenes [23], or text mining [24]. In contrast, it is a challenging task to obtain weights learned in advance as transfer learning because of the use of original sensors for this study. Therefore, we compared traditional machine learning algorithms used for a recognizer; such algorithms are used widely before the dissemination of deep learning.

Comparison algorithms are of eight types: Gaussian Naive Bayes (GNB) [26], AdaBoost (AB) [27], k-Nearest Neighbor (kNN) [28], Stochastic Gradient Descent (SGD) [29], Support Vector Machines (SVMs) [30], Logistic Regression (LR) [31], Gradient Boosting Decision Tree (GBDT) [32], and Random Forest (RF) [33]. We selected the best performance algorithm from the criteria of recognition accuracy and calculation speed with cross validation [34] using a similar dataset.

IV. Evaluation experiment

A. *Datasets*

The aim of this study is to realize a smart sensor system for monitoring elderly people for providing relief and safety combined with privacy and QoL using invisible sensors. As a benchmark dataset for evaluating the performance of our proposed system, sensor signals and Ground Truth (GT) labels are necessary for constructing a recognition model. Based on the main user for this system for this preliminary experiment, elderly people, we obtained monitoring datasets and their GT based on life records obtained from healthy university students who live in an apartment. The number of subjects was four persons in their 20s.

Before obtaining monitoring datasets, we underwent an ethics approval review by our university to obtain human data. After receiving approval, we orally explained the purpose and agreement of this research to subjects using a handout that contains the same contents. We prepared an installation manual for setting up the home agent and ambient sensors. After installation, we verified the respective systems in their residence using photographs taken using the camera of a smartphone. No particular difficulty was encountered related to installation or assignment.

All subjects wrote their life records used for GT with obtaining monitoring signals from respective sensors. The recording contents comprise event times of seven patterns: getting up, sleeping, going out, coming home, emergency calls, opening or closing of a refrigerator, and the use of a TV remote control. They used a format to write them with the resolution of minutes from a radio-controlled clock.

Herein, the consistency of life records depended on the respective subjects because for reasons of privacy, we did not use a camera at their residence. The subjects, rather than volunteering, joined this experiment as a part-time job to verify its correct function. If some readily apparent error was identified in terms of not getting up after sleeping, we modified the life record after confirming that fact with subjects.

We conducted a monitoring experiment divided into 2 periods of one month each. The first and second experimental periods were, respectively, from October 27 through November 25 and from November 29 through December 28, 2017. The respectively obtained datasets were defined as Datasets 1 and 2. Herein, Dataset 2 contains data loss because of malfunctions of the home agent and the server. Therefore, the data lengths of one subject and other three subjects were, respectively, 18 days through December 16 and 27 days through December 25. For learning, we used datasets stored in the server with offline signal processing without using the monitoring signals obtained directly from the home agents and the ambient sensors.

The recognition target patterns comprise three states: going out (Out), staying at home (Home), and sleeping on the bed (Sleep). In addition to these three patterns, our system can recognize the opening or closing of a refrigerator door and turning on or off a TV using a remote control from the life records used for GT. By contrast, to maintain the privacy of monitoring subjects, we set target patterns as the minimum necessary for recognition.

The reports [35]-[37] addressed that it is useful to confirm survival at home using an electric kettle, a TV, a microwave oven, and a refrigerator. We consider that unexpected accidents are preventable if a state change between Home and Sleep could be detected. Therefore, we set three states as the basic life patterns, which were the minimum necessary combination for the recognition of this monitoring experiment.

The time resolution was set to one minute intervals based on the figure reported by Mori et al. [38] for the number of sensor responses and the frequency of switching behavior statuses. For this experiment, 43,200 sensor signals were obtained as evaluation targets from each dataset of one month.

The model numbers of the four home agents, which transmit monitoring signals to the server through a mobile router, were M2001, M2002, M2003, and M2004. The discretized sensor signals were displayed each day on a web page as color bars. With consideration of privacy, the visualization range is set to 15 hours from 6:00AM to 21:00PM. By contrast, we used the whole 24 hours of signals for the evaluation of identified life patterns with 10-fold cross validation. For instance, signals of 27 days and 3 days in 30 days were, respectively, divided into training and validation sets with exchange 10 times.

B. *Comparison of learning algorithms*

Using Dataset 1, we conducted a comparison experiment with learning algorithms. Table I presents comparison results of mean accuracies of ten trials with cross validation. Recognition accuracies except for those GNB and AB were approximately 80%. In the remaining eight learning algorithms, the recognition accuracy of GBDT was 83.72% as the highest accuracy.

Table II depicts results of the processing time for the respective algorithms. As computer hardware, this study used a 2.6 GHz Intel Core i 5 CPU with 8 GB of 1600 MHz DDR

TABLE I. COMPARISON RESULTS OF MACHINE-LEARNING ALGORITHMS [%]

Algorithms	M2001	M2002	M2003	M2004	Average
GNB	72.82	59.90	49.09	48.79	57.65
AB	59.55	71.79	72.26	57.43	65.26
kNN	80.28	84.11	68.43	83.87	79.17
SGD	81.90	87.18	72.35	78.35	79.95
SVM	80.28	86.01	**76.03**	80.00	80.58
LR	83.04	87.91	73.48	80.30	81.18
GBDT	85.28	**92.23**	72.16	**85.20**	**83.72**
RF	**85.94**	91.95	72.50	84.06	83.61

TABLE II. COMPARISON RESULTS OF PROCESSING TIME IN EACH ALGORITHMS [SEC]

Algorithms	M2001	M2002	M2003	M2004	Total
GNB	**0.66**	**0.62**	**0.64**	0.75	2.68
AB	26.48	29.09	27.03	26.41	109.01
kNN	2.80	3.07	2.76	4.69	13.31
SGD	0.67	0.63	0.70	0.68	2.67
SVM	23.95	24.35	26.87	29.93	105.11
LR	2.20	2.27	2.47	2.37	9.32
GBDT	52.45	51.08	48.73	41.94	194.20
RF	0.67	0.66	0.70	**0.60**	**2.62**

3 main memory. The operating system was macOS Sierra version 10.12.6. We used Python's open-source machine-learning library scykit-learn [39] from a command line without using graphics. The processing time was measured as software time using a standard function on Python.

As depicted in Table II, the minimum execution time was 2.62 s for RF. The comparison result denotes that NG and SGD have similar processing speeds. Herein, the processing time of GBDT was 194.20 s, which was 86.93 times longer than that of RF. By contrast, the difference of mean recognition accuracies was merely 0.11%. We selected RF as an algorithm for life pattern recognition for this study.

C. *Recognition results of life patterns*

For this evaluation experiment, we used all sensors because the amount of data traffic is small compared with image or sound data. Herein, the difference in recognition accuracies was evaluated as the combination of sensors used in preliminary experiments.

TABLE III. RECOGNITION ACCURACY FOR DATASET 1 [%]

No.	M2001	M2002	M2003	M2004	Average
1	76.84	91.53	84.81	91.87	–
2	97.34	88.82	92.78	96.10	–
3	98.74	99.43	83.01	96.60	–
4	99.35	99.05	99.35	93.30	–
5	85.39	99.05	60.97	87.01	–
6	89.08	97.57	82.31	86.36	–
7	95.24	98.72	67.27	82.41	–
8	91.64	92.91	66.98	79.60	–
9	59.85	98.29	82.58	85.99	–
10	65.90	54.12	4.91	41.34	–
Average	85.94	91.95	72.50	84.06	83.61

TABLE IV. RECOGNITION ACCURACY FOR DATASET 2 [%]

Term	M2001	M2002	M2003	M2004	Average
18 days	95.72	92.49	86.11	95.80	92.53
27 days	98.10	94.77	88.69	–	93.85

Table III presents recognition accuracies for Dataset 1. The recognition accuracies for 10 sets of the cross verification are shown as detailed results. The mean recognition accuracy of the four subjects was 83.61%. Details reveal that the highest and lowest recognition accuracies were, respectively, 91.95% for M2001 and 72.50% for M2002. Herein, the recognition accuracies of some subjects were extremely low, as revealed in the details of cross validation results. For this experiment, we evaluated the result as mean accuracy, not merely obtained highest accuracy in the combination of the cross validation. Herein, the low recognition accuracy of M2003 was cased from GT as handwritten life records because the subject sometime forgot to record it.

Table IV presents recognition accuracies for Dataset 2. For this dataset, data deficits were found from malfunctions related to the home agent and the server. Because of the malfunction of the home agent, the mean recognition accuracy for the 18-day monitoring period was 92.53%. Compared with the result on Dataset 1, the mean recognition accuracy improved 8.92% with the effect of the shortened period. To alleviate trouble, we changed M2004 to M2005, which was an alternative home agent. However, the problem of sensor signal monitoring continued. After terminating the receipt of data related to this subject, we continued monitoring for three subjects from the 19th day. The mean recognition accuracy for the partial dataset collected up to 27 days until the server trouble was 93.85%. Although monitoring terms and subjects were insufficient, the former and latter results were, respectively, 8.92% and 10.24% higher than that of Dataset 1.

V. CONCLUSION

This paper presented a novel life monitoring system consisting of a home agent and ambient sensors. As a preliminary experiment aimed at monitoring various life patterns of elderly people, we conducted a monitoring experiment during two months for four university students subjects in their 20s. We developed a recognition method for three life patterns using machine-learning algorithms. Experimentally obtained results revealed that the mean recognition accuracy was 83.61% for Dataset 1, which was obtained from the first half of the monitoring experiment during one month with one-minute downsampled signal intervals. For the last half of the monitoring experiment, data acquisition was interrupted because of a malfunction of the home agent. We continued the evaluation experiment of life patterns with delimiting two periods. The recognition accuracies were 92.53% for 18 days and 93.85% for 27 days in Dataset 2.

For our future work, we expect to consider stable operation of the whole system and prompt responses to malfunctions, if they should occur. Moreover, we would like to increase the number of recognition targets for daily behavior patterns while protecting privacy. Particularly, we would like to realize a new emergency notification function using a pillow sensor. Furthermore, after the cooperation with single elderly people for extending systemization and practical application, we hope to conduct demonstration experiments.

ACKNOWLEDGMENT

This study was conducted with the support of the Ministry of Internal Affairs and Communications, Strategic Information and Communications R&D Promotion Program (SCOPE 152302001) in Japan. We are grateful to Prof. Katsumi Wasaki and Assoc. Prof. Masaaki Niimura of Shinshu University for helpful discussions related to this study as our joint study project.

REFERENCES

[1] H. Tanaka and S. Morizane, "A Study on Initiatives by Housing Complex Residents' Associations for Preventing Elderly from Experiencing Solitary Death," Japan Academy of Community Health Nursing, vol. 19, no. 1, pp. 48–54, 2016. (in Japanese)

[2] Q. Ni, A. Hernando, and I. Cruz, "The Elderly ' s Independent Living in Smart Homes: A Characterization of Activities and Sensing Infrastructure Survey to Facilitate Services Development," Sensors, vol. 15, pp. 11,312-11,362, 2015

[3] F. Ozaki, "A Survey for the Research Status of Elderly Care Robots," Memories of Shonan Institute of Technology, vol. 48, no. 1, pp. 21–32, 2013. (in Japanese)

[4] T. Miyake and T. Hatsukari, "Nursing Bed and its Peripheral Equipment," Journal of the Society of Instrument and Control Engineers, vol. 56, no. 5, pp. 371–376, 2017. (in Japanese)

[5] C. R. Petersen, "Mild Cognitive Impairment," Continuum: Lifelong Learning in Neurology, vol. 22, no. 2, pp. 404–418, 2018.

[6] Y. Sumi, "Evaluation Criteria and Methods of Robotic Care Devices in the Case Example of Mimamori (Watch-over) Sensors," Journal of the Robotics Society of Japan, vol. 34, no. 4, pp. 240–243, 2016. (in Japanese)

[7] Y. Ho, E. S. Shimokawara, K. Wada, T. Yamaguchi, and N. Tagawa, "Developing a life rhythm related human support system," Proc. IEEE 24th International Symposium on Industrial Electronics, pp. 894–899, 2015.

[8] T. Morishita and S. Mochida, "Simple Observation Sensor System and Local Community Network Model: Real Society Experiment on Solitary Death Prevention for Low-Income Single Elderly Residents in Collective Housing," Artificial Life and Robotics, vol. 22, no. 3, pp. 289–295, 2017.

[9] Y. Jiang and J. Liu, "Health Monitoring System for Nursing Homes with Lightweight Security and Privacy Protection," Journal of Electrical and Computer Engineering, Article ID 1360289, 2017.

[10] S. Park, M. Subramaniyam, S. Hong, and D. Kim, "Service Based Healthcare Monitoring System for the Elderly - Physical Activity and Exercise," Proc. International Conference on Applied Human Factors and Ergonomics, Advances in Human Factors and Ergonomics in Healthcare and Medical Devices, pp. 337–342, 2017.

[11] T. Sumalan, E. Lupu, R. Arsinte, and E. Onaca, "Multipoint Wireless Network for Complex Patient Monitoring based on Embedded Processors," Proc. International Conference on Advancements of Medicine and Health Care through Technology, pp. 123–126, 2016.

[12] H. Ghayvat, S. Mukhopadhyay, X. Gui, and N. Suryadevara, "WSN- and IOT-Based Smart Homes and Their Extension to Smart Buildings," Sensors, vol. 15, no. 5, pp. 10350–10379, 2015.

[13] V. Mighali, L. Patrono, and M. L. Stefanizzi, "A Smart Remote Elderly Monitoring System based on IoT Technologies," Proc. International Conference on Ubiquitous and Future Networks, pp. 43–48, 2017.

[14] D. Riboni, C. Bettini, G. Civitarese, Z. H. Janjua, and V. Bulgari, "From Lab to Life: Fine-grained Behavior Monitoring in the Elderly ' s Home," Proc. IEEE International Conference on Pervasive Computing and Communication Workshops, pp. 342–347, 2015.

[15] D. Bacciu et al., "Detecting Socialization Events in Aging People: The Experience of the DOREMI Project," Proc. 12th International Conference on Intelligent Environments, pp. 132–135, 2016.

[16] D. Bacciu, P. Barsocchi, S. Chessa, C. Gallicchio, and A. Micheli, "An Experimental Characterization of Reservoir Computing in Ambient Assisted Living Applications," Neural Computing and Applications, vol. 24 no. 6, pp. 14511464, Springer-Verlag 2014

[17] D. Roggen et al., "Opportunistic Human Activity and Context Recognition," Proc. IEEE Computer Magazine, vol. 46, no. 2, pp. 36–45, 2013.

[18] K. Wasaki, M. Niimura, and N. Shimoi, "A Multi-agent Approach to Smart Home Sensors for the Elderly Based on an Open Hardware Architecture: A Model for Participatory Evaluation," Proc. Seventh International Conference on Simulation and Modeling Methodologies, Technologies and Applications, pp. 386–391, 2017.

[19] H. Madokoro, N. Shimoi, and K. Sato, "Unrestrained Multiple-Sensor System for Bed-Leaving Detection and Prediction," Nursing and Health, vol. 3, no. 3, pp. 58–68, 2015.

[20] T. Hatsukari, T. Shiino, and S. Murai, "The Reduction of Tumbling and Falling Accidents Based on a Built-in Patient Alert System in the Hospital Bed," Journal of Science of Labour, vol. 88, no. 3, pp. 94–102, 2012. (in Japanese)

[21] A. Krizhevsky, I. Sutskever, and G. Hinton, "ImageNet Classification with Deep Convolutional Neural Networks," Proc. Advances in Neural Information Processing Systems, vol. 25, pp. 1090–1098, 2012.

[22] Y. Guo et al., "Deep learning for visual understanding: A review, Neurocomputing, vol. 187, no. 26, pp. 27–48, 2016.

[23] B. Zhou, A. Lapedriza, J. Xiao, A. Torralba, and A. Oliva, "Learning Deep Features for Scene Recognition using Places Database," Advances in Neural Information Processing Systems, vol. 27, pp. 487–495, 2014.

[24] X. Sheng, X. Wu, and Y. Luo, "A novel text mining algorithm based on deep neural network," Proc. Inventive Computation Technologies (ICICT), International Conference on, pp. 1–6, 2016.

[25] S. J. Pan and Q. Yang, "A Survey on Transfer Learning," IEEE Transactions on Knowledge and Data Engineering, vol. 22, no. 10, pp. 1345–1359, 2010.

[26] H. Zhang, "The Optimality of Naive Bayes," Proc. Seventeenth International Florida Artificial Intelligence Research Society Conference, 2004.

[27] Y. Freund and R. Schapire, "A Decision-Theoretic Generalization of On-Line Learning and an Application to Boosting," Proc. Second European Conference on Computational Learning Theory, pp. 23–37, 1995.

[28] B. V. Dasarathy, "Nearest Neighbor (NN) Norms: NN Pattern Classification Techniques," IEEE Computer Society, 1991.

[29] J. Dean et al., "Large Scale Distributed Deep Networks," Proceedings of the 25th International Conference on Neural Information Processing Systems, vol. 1, pp. 1223–1231, 2012.

[30] V. Vapnik, Statistical Learning Theory, Wiley, 1998.

[31] D. Cox, "The regression analysis of binary sequences," Journal of the Royal Statistical Society: Series B, no. 20, pp. 215–242, 1958.

[32] J. H. Friedman, "Stochastic gradient boosting," Computational Statistics & Data Analysis, Elsevier, 2002.

[33] L. Breiman, "Random Forests," Machine Learning, vol. 45, no. 1, pp. 5–32, 2001.

[34] S. Arlot and A. Celisse, "A Survey of Cross-Validation Procedures for Model Selection," Statistics Surveys, vol. 4 pp. 40–79, 2010.

[35] S. Aoki, M. Onishi, A. Kojima, and K. Fukunaga, "Detection of a Solitude Senior's Irregular States Based on Learning and Recognizing of Behavioral Patterns," IEEJ Transactions on Sensors and Micromachines, vol. 125, no. 6, pp. 259–265, 2005. (in Japanese)

[36] H. Matusi, K. Nakajima, and K. Sasaki, "Development of Telemonitoring System to Monitor Television's Operating State between Families," Trans. Japanese Society for Medical and Biological Engineering, vol. 46, no. 1, pp. 117–123, 2008. (in Japanese)

[37] M. Tsuda, M. Tamai, and K. Yasumoto, "A Monitoring Support System for Elderly Person Living Alone through Activity Sensing in Living Space and Its Evaluation," Information Processing Society of Japan, vol. 2014–CSEC–64, no. 43, pp. 1–7, 2014. (in Japanese)

[38] T. Mori et al., "Life Pattern Estimation of the Elderly Based on Accumulated Activity Data and its Application to Anomaly Detection," Journal of Robotics and Mechatronics, vol. 24, no. 5, pp. 754–765, 2012.

[39] F. Pedregosa et al., "Scikit-learn: Machine Learning in Python," Journal of Machine Learning Research, no. 12, pp. 2825–2830, 2011.

Feasibility Experiment on Position Estimation of Various Sound Sources in Indoor Environment

Takeru Kadokura Shigenori Ioroi Hiroshi Tanaka
Course of Information & Computer Science
Graduate School of Kanagawa Institute of Technology
Atsugi-Shi, Kanagawa, Japan
email: s1885004@cco.kanagawa-it.ac.jp, {ioroi, h_tanaka}@ic.kanagawa-it.ac.jp

Abstract— **This paper describes a method for estimating the position of various sound sources in an indoor environment and presents the results of basic positioning experiments. To date, we have performed position estimation based on the Time Difference Of Arrival (TDOA) method. In this investigation, the reception time difference at each reception point is compared to the theoretical value using a diffused sound, the human voice, the sound made by an operating microwave oven, and the ringing of a telephone. The reception time difference is necessary for position estimation. The reception time difference was obtained by cross correlation processing. Then, although the sound source position was obtained using this result, satisfactory positioning accuracy was not obtained except for the diffused sound source. Therefore, the whitening cross correlation method called Cross-power Spectrum Phase (CSP) analysis was applied. As a result, we could obtain a more accurate time difference than simple cross correlation for all sound sources, and we obtained a prospect that high accuracy positioning is possible.**

Keywords-Indoor Positioning; Sound Source; TDOA; Cross Correlation; CSP Analysis.

I. INTRODUCTION

We have been studying a high-accuracy indoor positioning system using sounds. A special sound source that transmits ultrasonic waves [1] or diffused sound [2] as a sound source was used in this system. In this study, we experimentally investigated the feasibility of estimating the position of a sound source originating in an indoor environment, such as the human voice and the sounds made by electrical appliances.

If the location of these sound sources can be established, it should be possible to monitor the conversation environment in an office by combining it with speaker recognition technology, and can be used to monitor an operating situation of household appliances. By using the position information of the sound source, it should be possible to identify the position of operating household appliances with a high degree of accuracy by incorporating sound classification technology. For example, this could be applied to watching over an elderly person living alone by monitoring the usage of home appliances. The proposed technology would appear to have many potential applications. In addition to a diffused sound that is used in conventional positioning systems, the source position of the human voice, the sound a microwave oven makes while operating and the ringing sound of a telephone were investigated in this paper.

The rest of the paper is structured as follows. The Section 2 describes the differences between related work and this paper. The basic principle of our proposed method is shown in Section 3. In Section 4 and 5, we show the experimental results of detecting the reception time difference from various sound sources by the simple cross correlation, and the result of the positioning experiment using these time differences. It is shown that it is difficult to satisfy the target positioning accuracy. We apply the CSP analysis and show the result of obtained reception time difference in Section 6. By applying this method, we can detect the reception time difference with higher accuracy, and show that we got the prospect of high accuracy positioning. This may lead to privacy concerns, and it is considered necessary to discuss and examine from this viewpoint. However, this paper focuses on the technology for position detection and does not discuss the viewpoint of privacy.

II. RELATED WORK

In position estimation using sound, research is being conducted to obtain accurate position of the sound source. It uses ultrasonic waves [3] or a dedicated sound source [4] for positioning, thus a special sound source is necessary for use, which is an impediment to popularization. On the other hand, for many environmental sound sources, the estimation of arrival direction is investigated rather than the estimation of the position of the sound source. In these methods, for example MUltiple SIgnal Classification (MUSIC) method is proposed and the direction of arrival of sound is detected from the spatial spectrum called the MUSIC spectrum [5][6].

CSP analysis [7] is a method used for detecting the difference in time of arrival of acoustic waves from a sound source to two microphone sensors. Although a method of estimating the position of the sound source using this information has been proposed, the authors estimated the position by statistical processing or filter processing, and accuracy is about several tens of centimeters [8][9]. As far as we know, there are no cases where the realized high accuracy is about several cm using environmental sound source other than the dedicated sound source. This research aims to realize the accurate positioning of the sound source in indoor space without the ultrasonic wave or the diffused sound source.

III. Basic Principle of Proposed Method

The location estimation method which we have applied to date is based on the TDOA scheme. In our method, a special sound source is prepared and transmits a sound that has been diffused using an M sequence code. The receiving side has the same sound source data as that of the transmitting side (replica), and detects the sound reception timing by cross correlation calculation between the received signal and the replica. Positioning calculation is conducted by using the reception time differences for each receiver. The positioning is conducted by solving the following equation (1) using numerical computation. This equation for positioning is the same as that of Global Positioning System (GPS) / Global Navigation Satellite Systems (GNSS) in which the radio signals is used.

$$\begin{aligned}\sqrt{(x-x_0)^2+(y-y_0)^2+(z-z_0)^2} &= ct \\ \sqrt{(x-x_1)^2+(y-y_1)^2+(z-z_1)^2} &= c(t+t_1) \\ \sqrt{(x-x_2)^2+(y-y_2)^2+(z-z_2)^2} &= c(t+t_2) \\ \sqrt{(x-x_3)^2+(y-y_3)^2+(z-z_3)^2} &= c(t+t_3)\end{aligned} \quad (1)$$

where,

t : propagation time [s]

x, y, z : position of transmitter [mm]

t_i : propagation time difference to each microphone sensor [s]

c : speed of sound [mm/s]

x_i, y_i, z_i : installation position of each microphone sensor [mm]

In this investigation, we considered the human voice and several other sound sources, such as home electrical appliances, in an indoor environment. Therefore, it is difficult to implement a replica on the receiving side as it can be done when the conventional method is used. In the proposed method, the reception time difference is obtained by cross correlation between the signal received at the reference point and the signal at each reception point, as shown in Figure 1. Based on the reception time differences obtained with this configuration, positioning calculation is performed in the same manner as that in the conventional method.

IV. Reception Timing Experiment

The experimental setup is shown in Figure 2. A sound source was installed on the floor (in this case, the previously recorded sound source (WAV format) was reproduced by a speaker), and the time at which the sound was received (reception time) by each microphone sensor was obtained by correlation processing. The distance between the sound source and the microphone sensor was kept at about 1 m.

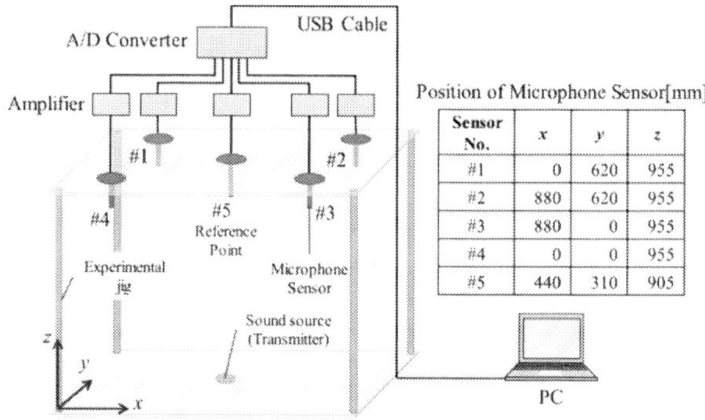

Sensor No.	x	y	z
#1	0	620	955
#2	880	620	955
#3	880	0	955
#4	0	0	955
#5	440	310	905

Figure 2. Experimental setup.

The received waveform (received at sensor (receiving point # 5) from the sound source) is shown in Figure 3. The sampling rate was 0.01 ms. The microphone sensors and speaker used in this experiment were the Primo EM-158 and Tang Band W2-858SB, respectively. The diffused sound source by the ninth order of the M-sequence code used in the positioning system we developed is also shown for comparison. The sounds of an operating microwave oven, a ringing phone and the human voice were examined in this investigation.

The blue line is the result for a diffused sound; the variations within a short time span can be attributed to the spread spectrum by chips (chip rate: 0.04 ms) of the M sequence code. The other signals, i.e., microwave oven and phone, are shown for the same time duration. It was confirmed that sound could be received by all microphone sensors.

Based on the received signal at sensor #5, the cross correlation with the received signal at each sensor was calculated for each sound signal. The cross correlation results for each sound source between sensors #5 and # 1 are shown in Figure 4 as one example. These results are obtained by the function "xcorr" of MATLAB.

The sound source diffused by M sequence code is the clearest and shows the cyclic peak of the correlation value. Peak position can be regarded as the time difference between

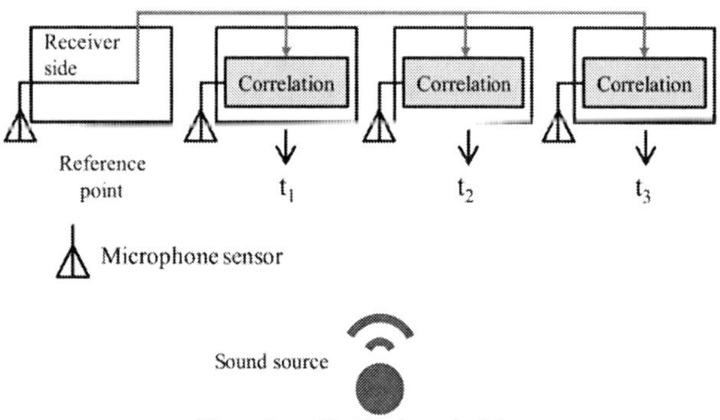

Figure 1. Positioning principle.

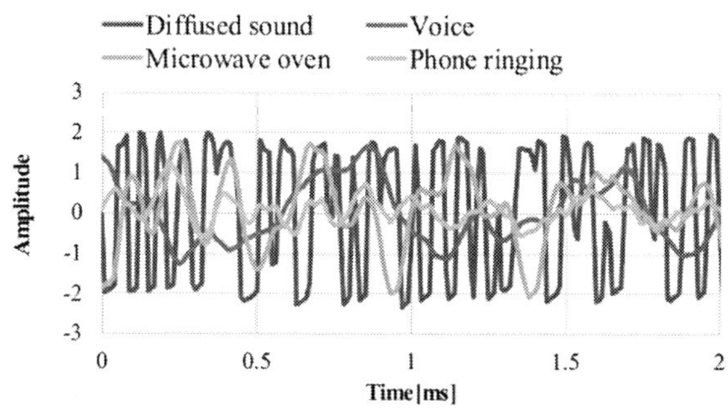

Figure 3. Received waveform.

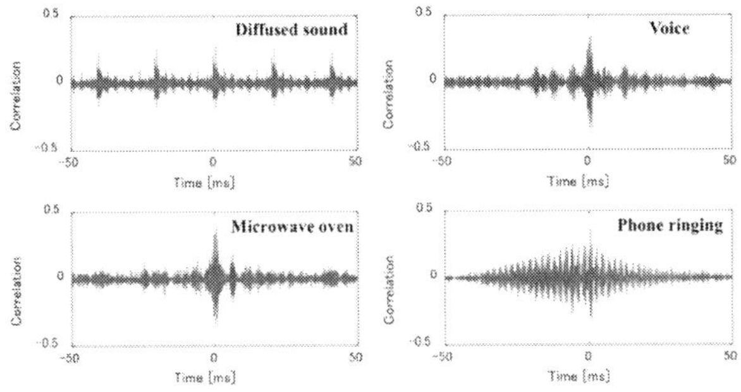

Figure 4. Example of cross correlation results.

two sound reception points. The correlation value can also be obtained from other sensors (receiving points).

We took 100 timings obtained from the peak position, and their average (μ) and standard deviation (σ) were evaluated before conducting the positioning experiment. In this experiment, the peak position, i.e., the time having the highest value, is considered to be the time difference. Table I shows the reception time differences obtained by correlation processing at each sensor as an evaluation of the reception time difference. As shown in Figure 2, the reception signals at sensors from #1 to #4 were used to calculate time difference and the signal at sensor #5 was used as reference. The theoretical value obtained from the sound velocity and distance between sensor #5 and each of the other sensors is shown in the right-hand column.

The differences between the experimental value and the theoretical values and the difference at each sensor result from the error of the peak position appearance caused by, for example, the effect of multipath signals or a low signal-to noise ratio of each of the sensors. The quality of the phone ringing was the worst in this experiment. Therefore, it seems to be difficult to get good positioning accuracy from the sound made by a phone.

V. POSITIONING RESULTS

The time difference values obtained by this method were used for the positioning calculation. Figure 5 shows the results of the positioning experiment obtained by correlation processing. The sound source was set at the center point (440, 310). As shown in Figure 2, it was confirmed that a positioning result closer to the center point can be obtained when the reception time difference is closer to the theoretical value.

As is clear from the result of the reception time difference, the sound source diffused by the M sequence, which is a

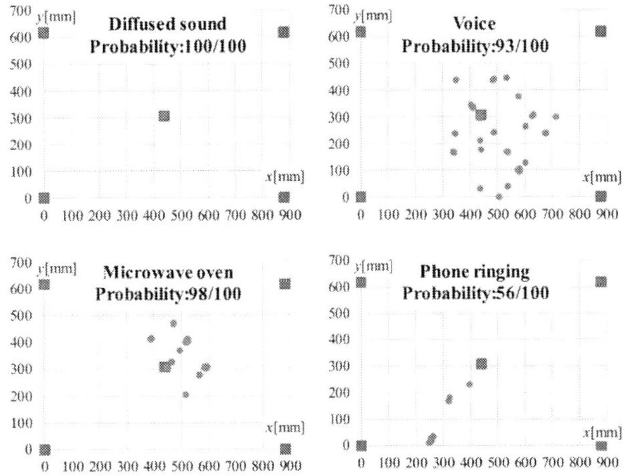

Figure 5. Positioning experiment results.

dedicated sound source used for positioning, gave the most accurate results. The numerical values in each graph, that is, the denominators and numerators in the graph, are the number of positioning times, and the number of times that the positioning result is within the range surrounded by the four reception points, respectively.

After the diffused sound, the sound generated by the operating microwave oven has the highest accuracy. Although the human voice can also be used to determine positioning, the error is significant. In this experiment, a microphone sensor was installed using a relatively small frame in order to construct an easy to use experimental system. The microphone sensors have been spaced at relatively narrow intervals of 620 mm and 880 mm. In practice, it is considered preferable for the microphone sensors to be placed at wider intervals from the viewpoint of installation load and cost. The time at peak position obtained from the correlation calculation, which governs the positioning accuracy, under a decrease in the reception intensity and in a multipath environment, is unclear. It would appear that the detection accuracy needs to be confirmed when widening the sensor interval.

The positioning error results for each sound source are summarized in Table II. In this table, the average value and the Root Mean Square (RMS) value in the x-y plane of positioning error of each sound source are shown for all 100 positioning times. Here, the average value and the RMS value, both results including and excluding the points outside the range of the four reception points, are shown. The RMS result

TABLE I. RECEPTION TIME DIFFERENCE IN EACH POINT

	Difference of Reception Timing[ms]								
	Diffused sound		Voice		Microwave oven		Phone ringing		Theoretical value (Temp.:25°C)
	μ	σ	μ	σ	μ	σ	μ	σ	
t_1	0.58	1.1E-18	0.99	3.1E-4	0.55	1.2E-4	0.98	9.8E-4	0.58
t_2	0.58	1.4E-6	0.66	2.9E-4	0.25	1.4E-4	0.70	1.5E-3	0.58
t_3	0.58	3.3E-6	0.61	1.8E-4	0.38	1.9E-4	1.21	2.8E-3	0.58
t_4	0.58	1.7E-6	0.62	2.3E-4	0.61	5.6E-4	0.89	1.3E-3	0.58

TABLE II. POSITIONING ERROR

	All measurement[mm]			Region within 4 points[mm]		
	x average	y average	RMS	x average	y average	RMS
Diffused sound	0.23	-0.39	1.52	0.23	-0.39	1.52
Voice	63.13	-122.1	224.36	68.06	-104.16	197.57
Microwave oven	127.15	35.34	380.88	100.30	36.40	130.75
Phone ringing	44.68	-42.84	2300.13	-182.50	-279.46	347.64

of phone ringing was 2300; this was because some solutions have extremely large error.

For products with large dimensions, such as microwave ovens, an accuracy of about several centimeters is not necessarily required. However, in the case of positioning for small objects, such as call buzzers or alarms and when controlling the moving objects with high accuracy, it is necessary to suppress the positioning error to less than several tens of centimeters. It is of the utmost importance to devise a method that is able to reduce the positioning error.

The positioning error seems to be caused by the error of reception time deference obtained cross correlation calculation shown in Table I. A more accurate detection of reception time difference is required to keep positioning accuracy.

VI. Results by CSP analysis

There is a method of detecting the reception time difference by CSP analysis [7]. This method is also called a whitening correlation method, and it is said that the time difference can be accurately detected even for a sound source which is not whitened different from a diffused sound source. Figure 6 shows an example of the result by the cross correlation method and CSP analysis. This result shows the possibility that the CSP analysis can detect the reception time difference more accurately.

Table III shows the result of obtaining the reception time difference by the CSP analysis for the same sound sources shown in Table II. Significant improvements in detection accuracy can be confirmed. Although a large error (2.36 ms) occurs in the detection of a part of phone ringing, this error can be removed as an abnormal value from other conditions, such as the reception range of sound waves. By using this analysis, improvement of the positioning accuracy can be expected. We will use this method for the detection of the reception time difference and plan to perform the positioning experiment.

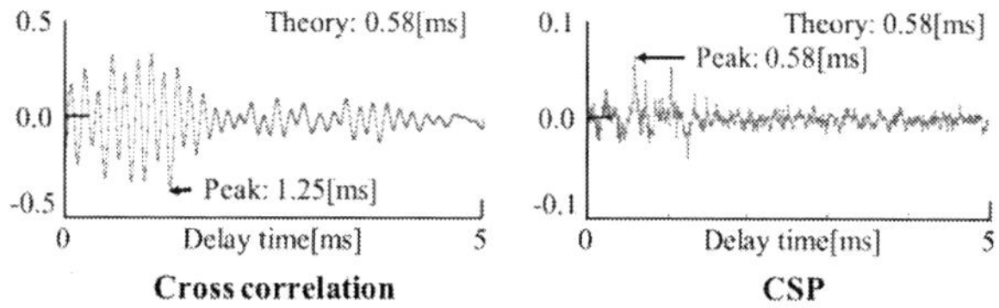

Figure 6. Difference of results by cross correlation and CSP analysis.

TABLE III. Reception time difference by CSP analysis

	Difference of Reception Timing[ms]								
	Diffused sound		Voice		Microwave oven		Phone ringing		Theoretical value (Temp.:25°C)
	μ	σ	μ	σ	μ	σ	μ	σ	
t_1	0.58	1.1E-18	0.46	6.6E-4	0.57	9.4E-5	0.59	1.0E-6	0.58
t_2	0.58	3.1E-6	0.57	1.3E-4	0.47	2.5E-4	0.57	1.0E-6	0.58
t_3	0.58	1.1E-18	0.57	1.4E-4	0.49	2.0E-4	0.56	3.9E-6	0.58
t_4	0.58	4.0E-6	0.55	1.8E-4	0.56	1.2E-4	2.36	1.3E-2	0.58

VII. Conclusion

We have experimentally examined a highly accurate positioning method for human voice, the sound generated by an operating microwave oven and a ringing phone. To date, sound source diffused by M sequence code is used for accurate indoor positioning in conventional systems. There would be numerous applications if other sound sources commonly present in indoor environments could be used for the positioning of a sound source.

Although the sound received timing used for positioning can be obtained by simple cross correlation calculation for each sound source, it was not possible to secure adequate positioning accuracy except for the diffusion sound source. For this reason, we conducted an experiment to find the accurate difference in reception time by applying the CSP analysis. As a result, the error of the reception time difference can be greatly reduced, and the prospect that the positioning with higher accuracy can be obtained. Future plans are to evaluate the positioning accuracy by using the time difference obtained by this method. Furthermore, it is necessary to evaluate the positioning accuracy with a more realistic configuration, that is, widening the installation intervals of the microphone sensors.

Acknowledgment

This work was supported by JSPS KAKENHI Grant Numbers JP17K00140.

References

[1] C. Yara, M. Akiyama, S. Ioroi, and H. Tanaka, "Indoor Positioning System using Ultrasonic Sensors as a Position Information Infrastructure for a Wide Area," Asian Conference on Information System 2013 (ACIS2013), pp. 386-389, 2013.

[2] K. Kaneta, M. Naruoka, S. Ioroi, and H. Tanaka, "Accurate Indoor Positioning using Sound with Distributed System Configuration," The Fifth Asian Conference on Information Systems (ACIS2016), pp. 114-120, 2016.

[3] A. Smith, H. Balakrishnan, M. Goraczko, and N. Priyantha, "Tracking Moving Devices with the Cricket Location System," ACM MobiSYS 2004, 13 pages, 2004.

[4] A. Mandal, C. V. Lopes, T. Givargis, A. Haghighat, R. Jurdak and P. Baldi, "Beep: 3D Indoor Positioning Using Audible Sound," Consumer Communications and Networking Conference, pp. 348-353, 2005.

[5] F. Asano, M. Goto, K. Itou and H. Asoh, "Real-time Sound Source Localization and Separation System and Its Application to Automatic Speech Recognition," Proc. of Eurospeech, pp. 1013-1016, 2001.

[6] P. Danes and J. Bonnal, "Information-Theoretic Detection of Broadband Sources in a Coherent Beamspace MUSIC Scheme," Proc. of IROS, pp. 1976-1981, 2010.

[7] D. Rabinkin, R. Renomeron, J. French and J. Flanagan, "Estimation of Wavefront Arraival Delay Using the Cross-Power Spectrum Phase Technique," 132nd Meeting of the Acoustical Society of America, pp. 1-10, 1996.

[8] M. Omologo and P. Svaizer, "Use of the Crosspower-spectrum Phase in Acoustic Event Location," IEEE Trans. on Speech and Audio Processing, vol. SAP-5, no.3, pp. 288–292, 1997.

[9] H. Okumura, K. Cho, T. Nishiura, Y. Yamashita, "Sound Source Localization Using a Distributed Microphones System," IEICE Technical Report, SP2006-139, pp. 61-66, 2007 (in Japanese).

Smart World: Convergence of Communication Networks and Enabling Technologies for Ubiquitous Services

Shaftab Ahmed
Department of Software Engineering
Bahria University, Islamabad, Pakistan
Email: Shaftab_2010@yahoo.com

Abstract – **The development of intelligent hardware and advancements in data communications networks have led to the development of smart technologies with Internet connectivity. Such devices are called Internet of Things (IoT) and are used to integrate intelligent solutions. The Service Oriented Architecture (SOA) has added virtuality, scalability, manageability, seamless cross platform communication and integration for ubiquitous availability. Mobile communication technologies have matured to 4G and 5G levels for global connectivity and use of satellite communications also called Wireless World Wide Web (WWWW). Progress towards 6G and 7G networks will address the difficulties of earlier standards, making space roaming a reality. Convergence of data communication paradigms is imminent due to advances in network technologies and evolving reliance on software defined networks. While the use of cloud computing and virtual storage is rapidly being accepted by computer users, the security of information particularly personal data and healthcare has to be improved. In this paper we review the enabling technologies of Next Generation Networks (NGN) for smart world and migration to IPv6 suit. In addition we discuss broadband access technologies merged with communications and network systems being used by enterprises, shopping complexes, healthcare systems, emergency response systems and traffic control.**

Keywords - SDN; wwww; SOA; IoT; BMS; WSN.

I. INTRODUCTION

Data communications and networking have become a life line of modern society. The world is experiencing a vital change due to the availability of smart solutions for all kinds of activities. The computation and data storage are not limited to desktop or central servers; instead the resources may be in virtual domain accessible through intelligent service providers. The services may also include the Quality of Service (QOS) and bandwidth on demand options available for prospective users.

The de-centralization of data storage and computation is the outcome of intelligent terminal equipment development and the use of computer networks. Internet revolutionized the Information Communication Technologies (ICT) activities by providing a gateway to users of all domains to share, communicate or use the data services offered by Internet service providers (ISPs). Service Oriented Architecture (SOA) has revolutionized the ICT activities leading to virtual storage, computation and a variety of service frameworks [1]. Cloud is the term used to describe virtual service paradigms, which use virtualized infrastructures to offer Software as a Service (SaaS) and Platform as a Service (PaaS) over Infrastructure as a Service (IaaS) allowing users to share physical resources in multitenant applications [2]. Network as a Service (NaaS) enables the use of heterogeneous hardware and software communication between devices and computers for exchange of information [3]. Software Defined Network (SDN) divides a computer network into Control Plane and Data Plane for better management and controllability through software.

Today we experience a convergence of technologies where smart phones, wireless sensors, laptops, tablets etc. are able to easily use the storage / computation services in virtual domain easily. The users of these Information Technology (IT) resources may not be professional computer scientists or engineers. The Internet of Things (IoT) architecture supports embedded sensors like Radio Frequency Identification (RFID) tags / reader, near field sensors (NFS), near field communication (NFC) and actuators [4]. The enormous amount of data from these devices has to be rationalized, processed, stored and presented in an easy to interpret form. Various solutions are available for this purpose however, custom tailored versions are preferred.

The mobile communication standards have evolved from 1G to 4G and now progressing towards 5G to 7G. The first generation (1G) was developed using analog systems available on Public Switched Telephone Networks (PSTN) and had a data rate of 2.4Kb/Sec. The second generation (2G) used digital data communication networks and technologies. The third generation (3G) is the outcome of success of 2G and is designed for user-user communication. It also laid down specifications of a framework for future growth of mobile communication technologies. The framework supports three tiers, i.e. Access technologies, Transport technologies and User applications [5]. The fourth generation (4G) was developed to integrate the cellular network technologies with Wi-Fi and fixed network technologies. The fifth generation (5G) increased flexibility in global communication systems to include satellite communications, hence, the evolution of wireless worldwide web (wwww) technologies [6]. The sixth generation (6G) is developed to overcome the problems of 5G, i.e. technology and standard variations in global communications systems [7]. The seventh generation (7G) will support space roaming through global integration of mobile communications with no data capacity and mobility restriction across countries and continents seamlessly [8].

Broadband access technologies, integrated with mobile communication platforms, will enhance the scope of distributed processing applications available for effortless usage through mobile applications [9]. Mobile application development is the fastest growing field in IT. Mostly Java programming language is used for application development and Java Virtual Machine (JVM) supports cross platform portability. The rest of the paper is organized as follows: in Section II we present relevant research work for IoT infrastructure development. In Section III, we discuss software and data network communication technologies in the context of smart world architectures. In Section IV, we present the challenges posed by IoT culture and the need to develop elaborate security mechanisms with forensic data management leading to enhanced and trustful usage of IoT devices. In addition we discuss future directions in security enhancements for IoT expansion in the context of distributed computing and data management involving Internet of things through hierarchical security policies.

II. RELATED WORK

Ubiquitous connectivity using Wi-Fi, Wi-Max and other similar technologies have supported the development of smart solutions for home / office automation, healthcare, guidance / surveillance systems, etc. Wireless sensors and actuators have led to the development of intelligent devices enabled to communicate over the web called IoT. The IT developers provide plug and play environments to integrate hardware and software for IoT. Hence, data acquisition, storage and sharing are effortless [10]. From a larger perspective, applications may collect measure and use the information for expert systems or Decision Support Systems (DSS). Convergence of technologies and the interests of IT developers, business communities and virtualization of multitenant, multiplatform architectures have extended the scope of service providers and IoT solution providers [11].

Social networking has become a means of evolving close knit communities. The registration, discovery and session management features allow interaction and usage of common resources through virtual networks abstracted through layered architecture. Ubiquitous services are available through hand held smart devices, which use wireless and fixed networks and communication systems in virtual domain. Distributed information systems are available to the users through converged IT solutions.

Healthcare support by intelligent data acquisition and management system has helped patients and doctors to avail all time connectivity, consultation and emergency response [29]. Home care systems have evolved where data periodically collected through sensors is measured, aggregated and sent to the servers / nursing stations where it is processed and saved in the personal history of the patients. Intelligent agents analyze the clinical data to monitor patients' progress and raise suitable alerts whenever required, under appropriate protocols and policies [36]. Alerts may be related to medicine intake, laboratory tests, exercise schedule, nutrition and procedures for treatment prescribed by the physician. In some cases, the alerts may be raised for imminent medical emergency, like heart attack or stroke, while the patient is unaware of the symptoms [37].

The growth of IoT and its integration in smart systems has increased vulnerability of digital systems. In prevailing security mechanisms, authentication, authorization and access control is extended to distributed data networks and eventually the cloud architectures. These systems have been developed as a result of research carried out in the last few decades to provide reasonably effective solutions in ICT industry. Data management in heterogeneous distributed systems accessible through smart systems with embedded IoT demand inclusion of new features for forensic studies.

Inclusion of intelligent devices capable to communicate with digital systems autonomously may cause serious security problems. Hence, new features like registration, verification and forensic data management are required for IoT in highly virtualized distributed systems in smart networks at home, neighborhood, city systems and the world at large. A home device authentication method based on Public Key Infrastructure (PKI) has been discussed in [12]. Light weight PKI has been proposed for mobile and hand held devices used in smart systems [13]. A model forensics aware system design for IoT in future systems has been presented by [14]. The concept of Certification Authority (CA) to maintain forensic information record about manufacturer code, unit number, seller / buyer / current owner identity along with password history, session key management trail with reasonable depth can be useful to make IoT security practical. Security information may be managed through hierarchical levels for quicker services and fault tolerance. The IoT may be linked to mobile, wireless and wired network networks with a possibility to extract trail of events for forensic study.

III. CONVERGENCE OF TECHNOLOGIES

Availability of broadband connectivity and multimedia support at affordable prices has merged data communications and computer networks. Developments of Wireless Sensor Networks (WSN) smart phones, hand held devices and intelligent host system developments have transformed the world into a digital society. IT applications range from home automation, healthcare, and education to industrial automation, environmental applications, e-government and smart city solutions. Increasing use of digital contents in data transmission over IP based networks has converged technologies in enterprises, homes and industry [10]. Virtuality is the popular way to integrate software, hardware and support systems into service oriented architecture (SOA). Out of these developments, a rapidly growing market of smart solutions has emerged [16].

Virtualization of computer hardware, software and services has led to integration of IT and Communication Technology (CT) for smart solutions. Wireless Internet aware intelligent technologies are rapidly becoming acceptable in human communities for various purposes. The evolving scenarios will allow integration of solutions by using interoperable IoT devices and Software Defined Networking (SDN). Figure 1 shows Next Generation Network (NGN) architecture based on layered model to integrate Original Equipment Manufacturers (OEMs), network technology developers, Telecommunication service providers, Radio / television and Internet Service Providers (ISP).

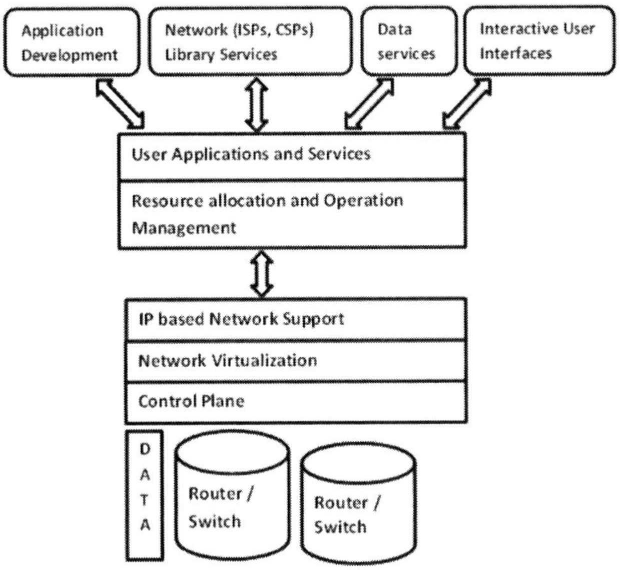

Figure 1. Convergence of network technolgies and the layered architecture over Software Defined Network (SDN)

Telecommunication companies and Radio/ Television are increasing use of Internet service model for all time and anywhere availability. Similarly the Packet switching, circuits switched to broad cast networks are offered through a common service layer, which uses protocol conversions, policy, Service Level Agreement (SLA). Converged networks require elaborate security, privacy and accountability policies for borderless communication [15].

Convergence of wireless, optical fiber and land based digital communication technologies with computer technologies for computation; data management and presentation etc. have ignited innovative growth of smart devices and applications in everyday life. The smart cities, smart enterprises / buildings, disaster management, medical / eHealthcare, smart grids and road traffic are the realms of the smart world [16][17]. We discuss the enabling technologies, network communication protocols and the security issues stemming out as a result of private and personal engagement through social networking [18][19].

A. Technical perspective

Smart data communication technologies have promoted easy integration of hardware and customized software solutions for distributed systems. The middleware support vendor neutral, platform independent hardware / software interface required to meet standards of interoperability, portability, transparency, mobility etc. We discuss example of smart city supporting eHealthcare, building management, road traffic and smart grids as under:

i. Smart City Management Systems (SCMS)

The smart solutions for everyday life as well as professional and industrial systems have given birth to the concept of "smart city". It is implemented through layered architecture where physical spaces, buildings, enterprises, transport utilities etc., are abstracted into city systems layer through ICT infrastructure [20]. These systems provide access to latest information concerning the city through Internet to be used for analysis and decision support systems. SOA has helped in making city systems ubiquitous and pervasive [21][22]. Convergence of networks plays a key role in seamless access to resources irrespective of software, hardware, and service platform. Network services play a key role by hiding platform and network layers in allowing access to resources.

ii. Building Management Systems (BMS)

Most of the enterprise buildings today have computer networks, which support services like database / document management, ecommerce, paging, video coverage along with Internet access. Intelligent building management systems are supported by IoT devices for autonomous data collection and submission to server; they may share data with other IoT devices in the neighborhood [23][24]. Electric power management of illumination lights, room air-conditioning and other activities can be handled by smart devices in coordination with server under a policy [25]. Ubiquitous cloud services may be used to provide anywhere, anytime availability of information. Smart city projects can be extended to integrate features offered by building management systems for various purposes like security and remote monitoring / management. A cyber-home connected to a service provider over the Cloud architecture is shown in Figure 2.

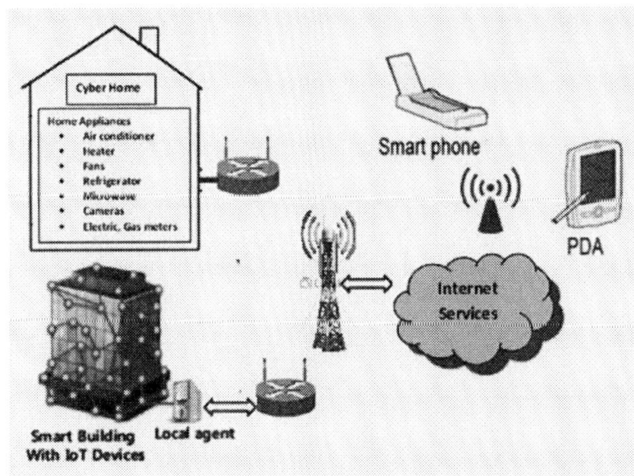

Figure 2. IOT: Smart Buildings and home architecture [Internet clipart resources]

Information sharing requires security features to be implemented in a building management system to avoid malicious activities. The IoT device authentication at home or office can be implemented by a hierarchical PKI based stack where the

Certification Authority (CA) at various levels plays a key role [25-28].

iii. *Medical and Healthcare Systems (MHS)*

Home care and e-Healthcare models are being rapidly developed to provide better quality of life, protection and health monitoring services. The aged or disabled people, patients getting prolonged medical treatment or requiring post-surgical monitoring are the clients for smart homes and smart cities. User friendly Decision Support Systems (DSS) over the cloud architecture allow the doctors to interactively make medical therapy schedule while getting patient's inputs on line if required [29]. Doctor's prescription for clinical tests, reports and patient monitoring may be managed online [30]. The IT and clinical tools are used for data searching and presentation to patients, doctors, pharmacists and researchers. Proactive monitoring of lab reports and the record of exercise / physiotherapy schedules is done by intelligent agents embedded in these systems. Figure 3 shows a typical e-Heathcare system using IoT devices.

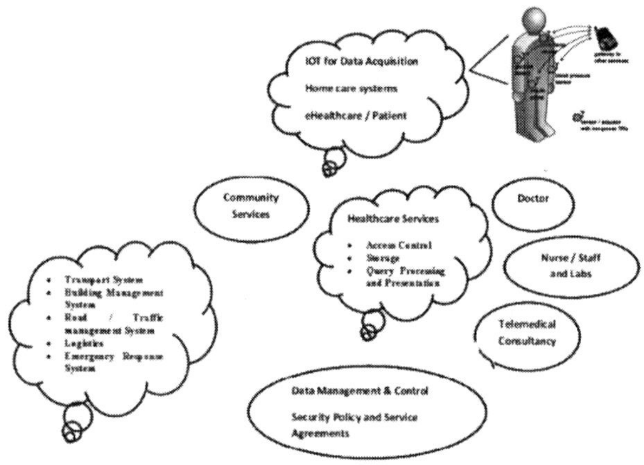

Figure 3. An e-Healthcare system using IoT devices

iv. *Intelligent transport systems (ITS)*

The industrial developments and availability of opportunities for technical financial and social growth has led to concentration of human population in big cities. Transport management in such cities is quite complex on account of varying traffic conditions, road accidents, etc. Conventional traffic control is supported by intelligent transport systems by using statistical record and live information for traffic forecast and raising alerts. The information is presented for traffic management and driving support through telecommunication system. The drivers can get traffic information on line while in transit or at home through intelligent devices and alerts. The emergency support systems along with multimedia services may be of great value for the commuters in many situations. Besides access to network services they may be able to communicate with other vehicles on the road. The fiber cables laid alongside long haul highways provide high speed data access through access points for wireless communication. Intelligent transport system consists of navigation, electronic toll collection, driving safety etc. [31][32]

B. *Enabling technologies for convergence*

Network hardware and software systems use technologies, which support interoperability and easy configurability through software. Object oriented programming tools are extensively used for this purpose. JAVA supports better portability across hardware and software platforms by using Java Virtual Machine (JVM) at an intermediate layer. It has won wide acceptability particularly for hand held smart devices using embedded operating systems like IOS, Tiny Linux, Android etc. Enabling technologies for convergence of IT activities are discussed as under:

i. *Smart devices and IoT culture*

Internet has been widely accepted norm of the modern world making it a global village engulfed into a virtual reality. The IoT culture and use of smart devices over available network solutions will add new dimensions to the social systems covering all areas of social, cultural and technical activities [33]. Wireless sensor networks often use low power, maintenance free devices at the front end and Wi-Fi, Wi-Max or land based communication systems for data network. IoT devices use wireless sensors for autonomous data collection, decision making and reporting events to servers under a policy.

ii. *Social Networking*

The participation of humans of all ages, professions and interests has given rise to formation of cyber communities spanning over computer networks. Community is a group of users sharing common interest for example content creators, users, developers and service providers, etc. form a group [34]. Hence, a community in the ICT domain may be seen as interlinked web pages in the Internet cloud. These communities are usually able to interact with each other hence, making bigger picture of social networking. Social networks like LinkedIn, Facebook, Twitter, WhatsApp, etc. have assumed importance for sharing information in professional and social groups or communities. Whereas it is an interesting phenomenon, it is often complicated and dangerous [35].

iii. *Cloud Services Architectures (CSA)*

An integrated e-Healthcare solution over cloud services architecture may be developed by utilizing web engineering technologies, coupled with software utilities of Hadoop Distributed File System (HDFS) along with a suitable RDBMS (Relational Database Management System) over high speed data communication infrastructure. The characteristics of ubiquitous healthcare system over a cloud should provide inexpensive, flexible, and reliable fault tolerant services [36][37].

iv. *Software Defined Network (SDN)*
Smart solutions offered through ubiquitous network connectivity and the evolving new paradigms the Internet of Things, smart cities and e-government demand fundamental changes in the network design techniques [38]. Application developers require intelligent management of networks for cloud services architectures hence, SDN is being used for flexibility, scalability and network management.

C. *Secure communication protocols*

It is estimated that 20 billion IoT devices will be attached to the Internet through ISPs in the next decade [24]. Extensive use of IoT devices will increase vulnerability due to a wider platform open to hackers and their malicious activities. The large number of devices requires low level identification / verification to conceive reasonable security architecture. Hence, a quick transition to Internet Protocol version 6 (IPv6) will be required to meet the enormous increase in devices, data and the handshake for secure communications [39]. The devices will be connected in a hierarchy of levels to reduce the overhead of protocol data and communication.

IV. CONCLUSIONS AND FUTURE DIRECTIONS

The software design and network architectures have to provide solutions for secure data sharing in multitenant domains. Service oriented computing offered in the cloud architectures use virtualized infrastructures to offer Infrastructure as a Service (IaaS) allowing users to share physical resources in multitenant applications.

Computer forensics can be summarized as the process of identifying, collecting, preserving, analyzing and presenting the computer-related evidence in a manner that is legally acceptable by the court of law. Integrity of information through verifiable procedures allows forensic data to be used for evidence. Forensics Aware IoT (FAIoT) [40][41] suggests three layers i.e. Cloud forensics, Network forensics and Device forensics for this purpose. The model is highly distributed hence, a trusted repository may be used for data collection, analysis and evidence extraction. An evidence collection module will monitor all registered IoT devices and store in the repository. To handle such large repository Hadoop Distributed File System (HDFS) has been proposed.

Internet based central registration of IoT for forensics through hierarchy of certification authorities (CA) can be used for security and verifiability. The typical PKI algorithm with some modifications to reduce overheads can be used for this purpose. The certificate may maintain security vectors for manufacturer, buyer, owner history, password history, GIS location etc. distributed at various levels. Secure session logs after TLS handshake at the Internet level can be maintained for forensic studies

REFERENCES

[1] H. Yoshida, R. Take, H. Kishimoto and Y. Hibi, " Service Oriented Platform" Fujitsu Sci.Tech. J. Vol 46, no. 4, pp 410-419, October 2010.

[2] R. Guha and D. Al-Dabass, "Impact of Web 2.0 and Cloud Computing Platform on Software Engineering" International symposium on electronic system design" 978-0-7695-4294-2/10, IEEE, DOI 10.1109/ISED.2010.48.

[3] W. Gerhardt, C. Cordero, C. Reberger and T. Dolan, "Mobile Network as a Service A New Solution Architecture for Mobile Network Operators" Cisco Internet Business Solutions Group (IBSG), March 2013.

[4] H. Farhady, H. Lee and A. Nakao "Software-Defined Networking: A survey" 1389-1286/_ 2015 Elsevier B.V. All rights reserved, pp79-95, 2015

[5] J. Kremer, "White Paper Near Field Commmunications" JKCS Consulting Services.

[6] M. Farooq, M. I. Ahmed and U. Mohammad, "Future Generations of Mobile Communication Networks" Academy of Contemporary Research Journal V II (I), 24-30, ISSN: 2305-865X, Resource Mentors (Pvt) ltd, 2013.

[7] J. Sen, " Convergence & Next Generation networks" Whitle paper, Tata Consultancy Services Ltd., Global ICT standardization forum for india (GISFI), Jul 2009

[8] J. Alleman and P. Rappoport, "The unsustainability of access competition ITU", The Future of Communications in Next Generation Networks, 15-16 January 2007.

[9] X. Li, A. Gani, R. Salleh and O. Zakaria, "The Future ofMobile Wireless Communication Networks" 978-0-7695—3522-7,IEEE Computer Society, DOI 10. 1109/ICCSN. 2009. 105.

[10] R. C. Huacarpuma et al," Distributed Data Service for Data Management in Internet of Things Middleware" Sensors 2017, 17, 977; doi:10.3390/s1705097 .

[11] J. Lopeza, R. Riosa, F. Baob and G. Wang, "Evolving Privacy: From Sensors to the Internet of Things, Journal of Future Generation Computer Systems May 29, 2017.

[12] D. Lee, J. Han and Y. Lee, "Home Device Authentication Method Based on PKI", , vol. 02, no. , pp. 7-11, 2007, doi:10.1109/FGCN.2007.143

[13] H. Jin and H. Chen, "Lightweight Session key Management scheme in Sensor Networks" FGCN '07 Proceedings of the Future Generation Communication and Networking - Volume 02 pp 3-6, ISBN:0-7695-3048-6, doi>10.1109/FGCN.2007.159.

[14] Shalini, V. N. Singh, M. Yadav and P. Rastogi, "Forensic Approach for Data Acquisition of Smart Phones to Meet the Challenges of Law Enforcement Perspective" J Indian Acad Forensic Med. April-June 2015, Vol. 37, No. 2 ISSN 0971-0973A.

[15] M. T. Abdullah, R. Mahmod , A. A. Ghani, M. Z. Abdullah, and A.Bakar, "Advances in Computer Forensics" IJCSNS International Journal of Computer Science and Network Security", VOL.8 No.2, February 2008.

[16] M. Al-Hader and A. Rodzi," The smart City Infrastructure Development & Monitoring" Theoratical and Empirical Researches" number 2(11) / May 2009.

[17] Z. Alazawi, O. Alani, M. Abdljabar, S. Altowaijri and R. Mehmood, " A Smart Disaster Management System for Future Cities", WiMobCity'14, August 11, 2014, Philadelphia,USA. doi.org/10.1145/2633661.2633670.

[18] C. Cerrudo, "An Emerging US (and World) Threat: Cities Wide Open to Cyber Attacks" a white paper, IOActive, Inc., 2015.

[19] "Cyber Physical Systems – Situation Analysis" NIST: National Institute ofstandards and Technology, March 2012.

[20] L. Anthopoulos, "From Digital to Ubiquitous Cities: Defining a Common Architecture for Urban Development" IEEE Computer Society, ISBN: 978-0-7695-4149-5 doi>10.1109/IE.2010.61.

[21] T. Na and T. mA. Pardo, "Conceptualizing Smart City with Dimensions of Technology, People, and Institutions" Proceedings of the 12th Annual International Conference on Digital Government Research, Dg.o'11, ACM 978-1-4503-0762-8/11/06.

[22] J. Lee, S. Baik, and C. Lee, "Building an Integrated Service Management Platform for Ubiquitous Ecological Cities", Computer, vol. 44, no. , pp 56-63, June 2011, doi:10.1109/MC.2011.131.

[23] M. Batty et al, "smart Cities of the future" Eur. Phys. J. Special Topics 214, 481–518 (2012), doi: 10.1140/epjst/e2012-01703-3.

[24] J. Yu, M. Kim, H. Bang and S. Kim, "IoT as a applications: cloud-based building management systems for the internet of things" Multimedia Tools and Applications • July 2015 doi 10.1007/S11042-015-2785-0.

[25] L. Ngo, "Service-oriented architecture for home networks", TKK T-110.5190 Seminar on Internetworking 2007-3-4/5 Helsinki University of Technology, Finland.

[26] G. Meyer and A. Stander, "Cloud Computing:The Digital Forensics Challenge" Proceedings of Informing Science & IT Education Conference 2015, pp 285-299.

[27] L. Vrizlynn and L. Thing, " Cyber Security for A Smart Nation" ieeexplore.ieee.org/stamp/stamp.jsp?arnumber=7238277.

[28] D. Lillis, B. A. Becker, T. O'Sullivan and M. Scanlon, " Current Challenges and Future Research Areas for Digital Forensic Investigation" The 11th ADFSL Conference on Digital Forensics, Security and Law (CDFSL 2016), Florida, USA, May 2016, arXiv:1604.03850v1 [cs.CR].

[29] M. Hassanalieragh et al, "Health Monitoring and Management Using Internet-of-Things (IoT) Sensing with Cloud-basedProcessing: Opportunities and Challenges" IEEE International Conference on Services Computing, 978-1-4673-7281-7/15, DOI 10.1109/SCC.2015.47, 2015.

[30] S. S. Ponedal and M.Tucker,"UnderstandingDecision Support Systems" journal of managed care pharmacy jmcp 2002 vol. 8, no. 2.

[31] S. L. Suen, S. Henderson,"Aapplication of Intelligent Transportation Systems to Enhance Vehicle Safety for elderly and Less able travellers" 16th International Technical Conference on the Enhanced Safety of Vehicles , The National Academies of Sciences, Engineering, and Medicine, DOTHS808759 Volume: 1 pp. 386-94.

[32] J. Walker, "Intelligent Transportation Systems Report for Mobile, GSMA Connected Living Programme,GSM Association, 2015.

[33] P.C.Jain and K.P.Vijaygopalan, " RFID and Wireless Sensor Networks" Proceedings of ASCNT – 2010, CDAC, Noida, India, pp. 1 – 11.

[34] A. Elmagarmid, A. Samuel and M. Ouzzani, "Community Cyber Infrastructure Enabled Discovery in Science and Engineering" Computing in Science and Engineering 10(5):46 - 53 • October 2008.

[35] K. Malagi, A. Angadi and K. Gull, "Survey on Security Issues and Concerns to Social Networks" International Journal of Science and Research (IJSR), India Online ISSN: 2319-7064.

[36] C. Orwat, A. Graefe and T. Faulwasser, "Towards pervasive computing in health care – A literature review" BMC Medical Informatics and Decision Making 2008, 8:26 doi:10.1186/1472-6947-8-26.

[37] E. Sazonov, K. Janoyan and R. Jhac, "Wireless Intelligent Sensor Network for Autonomous Structural Health Monitoring, doi=10.1.1.99.4283

[38] "SDN and the Future of Service Provider Networks" Fujitsu Network Communications Inc., 2013.

[39] Jara1, L. Ladid and A. Skarmeta, "The Internet of Everything through IPv6: An Analysis of Challenges, Solutions and Opportunities" Journal of Wireless Mobile Networks, Ubiquitous Computing, and Dependable Applications, volume: 4, number: 3, pp. 97-118.

[40] D. Loomis and B. Wohnsiedler, " The 'Internet of Things' (IoT)– Opportunities and Risks" American Society of Safety Engineers , ASSE-15-744, Professional Development Conference and Exposition, 7-10 June, 2015.

[41] S. Zawoad and R. Hasan, "FAIoT : Towards Building a Forensics Aware Eco System for the Internet of Things" 12th IEEE International Conference on Services Computing (SCC), DOI: 10.1109/SCC.2015.46.

An Approach to Auto-Enhance Semantic 3D Media for Ambient Learning Spaces

David Bouck-Standen, Alexander Ohlei, Thomas Winkler and Michael Herczeg
Institute for Multimedia and Interactive Systems (IMIS)
University of Luebeck
Luebeck, Germany
email: [bouck-standen, ohlei, winkler, herczeg]@imis.uni-luebeck.de

***Abstract*—In this contribution, we present an approach in enhancing 3D objects, which are automatically reconstructed from semantic media in a cloud-based ambient platform. Due to the automatic background process of 3D reconstruction, the objects contain artifacts from the reconstruction process and are not aligned and not positioned well for direct use in mobile augmented reality apps, such as our InfoGrid system. The goal is to automate the process of enhancing these 3D objects. In our approach, we monitor users' interactions with a Web-based 3D editor. From these interactions, we derive constraints and show, that for our scenario these parameters can be generalized and applied to other 3D objects, in order to process them automatically in the background. This continues previous work and extends the Network Environment for Multimedia Objects (NEMO), a Web-based framework used as the technical platform for our research project Ambient Learning Spaces (ALS). NEMO is the basis for ALS and among other features provides contextualized access and retrieval of semantic media. In various contexts of ALS, compared to still images or video, 3D renderings create higher states of immersion. We conclude this article with a discussion of our findings and with a summary and outlook.**

Keywords-Mobile media; Web frameworks; Ambient Learning Spaces; 3D object editor.

I. INTRODUCTION

Today, people are living in a networked society within digitally enriched environments consisting of various individual interconnections between physical and digital spaces. Together with ambient and mobile technology, these play an important role and affect our being and acting in the physical world. This is also accompanied by the creation of technology-assisted environments, like through the creation, manipulation and visualization of 3D objects [1].

In our research project, with *Ambient Learning Spaces (ALS)* [2] we create ubiquitous learning environments that feature personal and collaborative learning spaces interconnecting learners with their personal digital media and the media of others. It is assumed and under current research that in context of schools and museums, the relatedness of body and spaces supports the learning process, in which ALS enables learners to interact with media. ALS enables learners to structure information themselves using ambient technology in Web-based applications, which are especially available in mobile contexts on personal smartphones. In this setting, 3D renderings empower imagination, creativity and learning compared to still images or video [3]. This seems to be fostering the construction of useful and sustainable knowledge. In our research projects funded since 2008 by the German Research Foundation (Deutsche Forschungsgemeinschaft, DFG), we developed an ALS framework to create mixed reality learning spaces where body and physical space are extended by digital artifacts in the form of media. These media in general and especially mobile and ambient media become carriers of information utilized in various learning contexts. Learners and instructors extend these media by digital properties to construct semantic media [4].

As the backend of ALS, we developed the *Network Environment for Multimedia Objects (NEMO)* as a technical foundation of ALS [5]. NEMO is a Web-based framework and storage for semantic media. It stores media, such as text, still images, video, 3D objects, animations, and audio extended by digital properties organized through ontologies. Using NEMO together with some of the applications from the ALS family provides a digital overlay for physical objects using these semantic media.

Media, such as still images and videos from users stored in NEMO, are used in automated background processes by NEMO to create 3D objects from these media without the need of user interaction [6]. In our approach, we use these 3D objects to enhance learner's experiences by placing them into context, e.g., with the application InfoGrid, with which Web-based Augmented Reality (AR) tours for smartphones can be experienced [7]. Due to the process of automatic 3D reconstruction, 3D objects contain unwanted residues or artifacts and do not align well for the use in AR. With 3DEdit, we enable users to enhance 3D objects manually [1]. 3DEdit is a Web-based editor, which runs on the ALS platform, interfaces with NEMO, and does not require the installation of 3D editing programs on a dedicated graphics computer system.

In this contribution, we continue our previous work [1] [6] and present our latest work on automating the process of enhancing these 3D objects. From the user's interaction with 3DEdit we derive constraints and parameters, which can be applied to other 3D objects, in order to process them automatically. In Section 2, we discuss related work. In Section 3, we illustrate the scenario for this work and in Section 4, explain the realization. In Section 5, we present the latest approach for automatic 3D object enhancement and conclude with a summary and outlook in Section 6.

II. RELATED WORK

The research field of the Semantic Web [8] is still of core interest. It yields "naturally" structured data about the world in a well-defined, reusable, and contextualized manner. The

NEMO framework is related to metadata-driven digital media repositories [9] but is different compared to conventional repositories by delivering more sophisticated features through the NEMO logic [1].

The research field of e-learning is strongly related to our work as well. Although contemporary approaches make use of semantic structures [10], the understanding of the purpose of e-learning systems in general focuses mainly on tracking the learner's performance, provide learning materials or manage and collect assignments [11]. In contrast, our work focuses on linking educational contents with the lifeworld (Lebenswelt) and thus engaging learners in communicative and collaborative processes by expanding the learning environment through contextualized, personalized, body- and space-related semantic media. For this purpose, NEMO provides means of connecting learning spaces inside and outside of schools, museums, urban spaces and natural habitats. ALS create a motivating environment, in which learning is able to flow and develop in whichever way and direction the learner's like to follow. These digitally augmented learning environments transpose learning from formal to informal learning. They interlace real-physical spaces of everyday life with digital augmentations that facilitate individual and collaborative learning [12].

The field of human-computer interaction with regard to 3D objects is of interest for this research. We have examined various implementations featuring 3D object editing, also in Web-based applications. The implementations studied have in common to provide features for advanced or professional users and are directed at creating and editing 3D objects. Performing manipulations needed for our scenario would require many complex steps of interaction and would not allow editing 3D objects in a touch-only application as needed in our learning scenarios.

With regard to automatically edit, enhance and orient 3D objects, Fu et al. [13] and also Jin et al. [14] presented related work focusing on placing 3D objects upright on a planar level. This approach gives interesting insight into the algorithmic perception of 3D objects. However, it relies on an equilibrium calculation based on discriminative attributes linking the shape to function, which is assessed by machine learning algorithms. As this method works well with complete and closed "man-made" 3D objects, the properties of these 3D objects do not match the ones of objects we receive from 3D reconstruction for complex natural environments.

III. Scenario

For the following scenario, apart from NEMO, we refer to our currently implemented and usable ALS applications. As a starting point for the scenario, school students already created semantic media during their excursions, using the Mobile Learning Exploration System (MoLES), a smartphone app featuring the task-based creation and gathering of media. From these media, NOC3D has already reconstructed 3D objects, as illustrated in our previous work [1]. These 3D objects are now accessible on the InteractiveWall, an installation of large multi-touch screens typically placed in school foyers or public museum spaces [4], giving access to semantic media and other applications.

After a field trip, Sarah, a 14 year old student prepares a short presentation of her findings from her field trip. For this task, she decides to use media she created with MoLES, one of the mobile ALS apps to collect data and media in the field. She logs on to the InteractiveWall located in the foyer at school. She browses through automatically transferred media from her mobile using swipe gestures on the multi-touch screen. She is surprised to discover that among her media, one sculpture she took photos of is meanwhile available as an automatically created 3D object. Using the InteractiveWall, she views the 3D object in full-screen mode, which is shown in an upright position and in a face-view. Sarah wants to incorporate the 3D object into her presentation. For this purpose, she uses 3DEdit, which is embedded into the InteractiveWall, and does some fine tuning of the orientation of the 3D object. After finishing, she is happy with the rendering and incorporates the 3D object into her presentation.

During the presentation, some of her classmates are astonished that they did not notice the sculpture themselves before. With the help of the mobile application InfoGrid, they are now able to take a closer look at it from all sides. They get curious through Sarah's presentation on what she thinks how the sculpture "Neighbors in Conversation" is related to the current topics off their project.

Later, Sarah is engaged in another school project and logs into the ALS Portal. She browses again through her media to find something suitable to use for the new project. As she

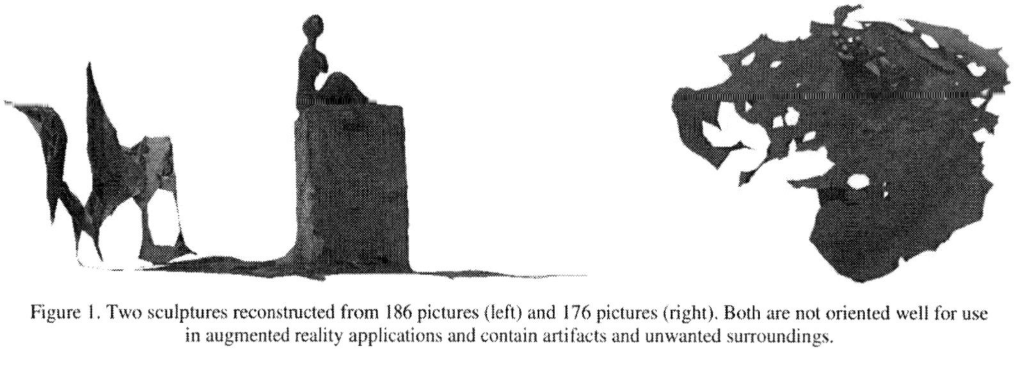

Figure 1. Two sculptures reconstructed from 186 pictures (left) and 176 pictures (right). Both are not oriented well for use in augmented reality applications and contain artifacts and unwanted surroundings.

Figure 2. Orienting (left) and cutting by placing a volume (right) in the web-based editor 3DEdit we used to monitor the subject's interactions.

comes across the sculpture of the "Neighbors in Conversation" she notices that a woman sitting on a bench is holding her child. She uses the 3D editor module inside the ALS Portal she used before on the InteractiveWall to cut out the child-holding woman to use this 3D element for her new project. She is satisfied that she can use the media again in a quite different context.

IV. REALIZATION

In ALS, we have implemented different components, which have been used as a basis for this work.

A. NEMO and 3D Object Reconstruction

NEMO is a Web-based framework for ALS. The NEMO API provides access for ALS learning applications [1][4]. The NEMO Converter 3D (NOC3D) extends NEMO Logic as a module. It runs in an autonomous mode as a background service without any user interaction required. All data processed are images and videos taken with different camera models. These are stored as semantic media in NEMO and selected by NEMO for the process of 3D reconstruction [6]. NEMO stores the reconstructed 3D object together with semantic annotations of the media used for reconstruction. These 3D object is now available for use through NEMO. Other ALS applications can now retrieve the 3D object, e.g., for further editing, or to view the object in various contexts, such as AR [7], as the scenario outlines.

B. Web-based 3D Editor

As NOC3D cannot determine which specific parts of the footage are relevant for the user, or the actual physical object, the reconstructed 3D objects may include superfluous parts of the physical object's environment, such as artifacts of the surrounding ground surface. Similarly, the desired focus of the object cannot be extracted reliably from the information available in semantic media. Thus, when viewed, the reconstructed 3D objects may appear with an offset to the side or turned away from the viewer (cf. Figure 1). The intuitive solution to isolate the physical object prior to reconstruction is not an option, as the process of 3D reconstruction requires surroundings to be part of the original footage [6].

For this reason, with 3DEdit we have developed a Web-based application, which offers functionalities to solve these issues for our scenario: (1) a function to cut extraneous parts of the 3D object and (2) a function to reorient the 3D objects, which sets the object's center and default orientation according to the user's requirements. 3DEdit (cf. Figure 2) offers a browser-based interface, which can also be used on the InteractiveWall or on mobile devices, like smartphones or tablets. Through this interface connected to NEMO, the necessary functionalities are simplified and automated to the point where they only require a single input by the user. The actual manipulation of the 3D object is conducted inside NEMO, so there is no special hardware required for this purpose.

The manual process of editing a 3D object is illustrated in Figure 2. In order to orient the misaligned 3D object (cf. Figure 2, left), the view is rotated until a suitable angle is found. This angle depends on the use case, in which the 3D object is used. Through experiments, we found that rotating the object toward a head-on view is sufficient for our scenario. Unwanted surroundings can be removed by placing a clipping volume around the area of the object to keep (cf. Figure 2, right). Any polygon outside the volume will be omitted or cut along the selected edge. After the 3D object is aligned and all unwanted surroundings and artifacts have been removed in the editor of 3DEdit, the backend of 3DEdit takes the necessary actions to calculate the final 3D object [1].

V. AUTOMATING 3D OBJECT ENHANCEMENT

We have introduced a technical solution to make the results of the automatic 3D object reconstruction in NEMO usable in other applications, such as the AR app InfoGrid. To achieve this, with cutting and orienting 3D objects we have identified two tasks we simplified into dedicated functions into 3DEdit, which do not require the complexity and extent of user interactions like typical 3D editors.

Now our goal is to fully automate the steps in order to enhance 3D objects. For this, we need to automatically (1) detect unwanted surroundings and (2) fix the orientation of the object and (3) perform the process of cutting and rotation.

At first, in the following section we conduct an analysis of the 3D objects at hand and compare our setting with related work in terms of compatibility. In Section V.B, we focus on our setting, in which we monitor interactions of 31 subjects with 3DEdit. In Section V.C, we detail our observations from the monitoring setting and in Section V.D, derive constraints to develop an automated algorithm for our goal.

A. Analysis

At first, a general classification of the 3D objects we receive from NEMO is necessary before proceeding further. In our ongoing research project, all NEMO-generated 3D objects have in common to be of a minimum of 15 cm and a maximum of 2.5 meters in height and width. The figures inside the 3D object can be classified as statues or of similar shape, meaning that the figures are generally standing on a planar surface and this surface is part of the 3D object. The figures are standing freely, which means they are not part of a larger coherent construction (cf. Figures 1-2). Consequently, these 3D objects have a base or similar, stand in an upright orientation. Additionally, sculptures typically have a front side, which can be found by rotating around the vertical axis in an upright perspective.

In the ideal case, the artifacts from reconstruction are only small parts of the objects, but from the experimental reconstruction of a total of 51 real objects we find found out that most reconstructed 3D objects differ from the ideal case, as illustrated in Figures 1-2. We have not defined a measure for the amount of artifacts, but they contain a considerable amount of artifacts, which do not belong to the figure to be preserved inside its digital representation.

The approaches of the related work analyze the given 3D objects by geometrical and other mathematical means [15]. In these approaches, shapes and orientation are analyzed and abstracted into orientation candidates, e.g., according to static equilibrium [13]. For each candidate, a set of discriminative attributes link the shape to function. In this approach, an assessment function of these attributes is learned from a training set using a combination of Random Forest and Support Vector Machine classifiers [13]. As the reconstructed 3D objects however may contain artifacts that are actually larger than the preferable figure itself, this algorithm cannot be used.

In this ongoing work, our approach is to monitor user interactions for typical patterns and derive constraints for 3D objects that yield heuristics, which we can transform into parameters for the automation of 3D object enhancement. Thus, in the following, we describe the setting, in which we monitored the users of 3DEdit in an evaluation with a total of 31 subjects.

B. Monitoring Setting

We conducted the monitoring of user interactions in an evaluation setting, which corresponds to our scenario. We simultaneously validated the technical system of the integration of 3DEdit into NEMO. Concerning the use of 3DEdit in a school environment running on the InteractiveWall installed in, e.g., a crowded and noisy school foyer, it is crucial that the task of enhancing the 3D object is accompanied by comfortable and predictable interaction. For this reason, our evaluation strategy focuses on the intuitive stage and hence, apart from the minimal on-screen help and a short introduction, no instructions, explanations and demonstrations of the usage and functions or techniques were presented to the subjects. The subjects used computer systems provided by us and were free to choose between mouse, touch-pad or on-screen multi-touch interaction. 3DEdit runs in a Web-browser and logs every step of user interaction through NEMO. The software was deployed on our servers in a live multi-user setting. For this setting, we have chosen the 3D object illustrated in Figure 1 (right). The subjects had two tasks, which were to (1) remove artifacts from the 3D object and (2) rotate it into head view, as illustrated above. In the beginning, the subjects saw a short introduction explaining the system and their task description, which was displayed on-screen. From this view, they were directed to 3DEdit, which initially shows the 3D object in its default orientation and the on-screen help.

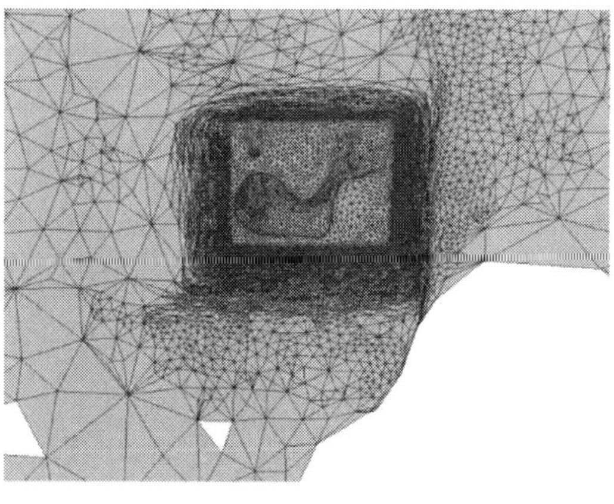

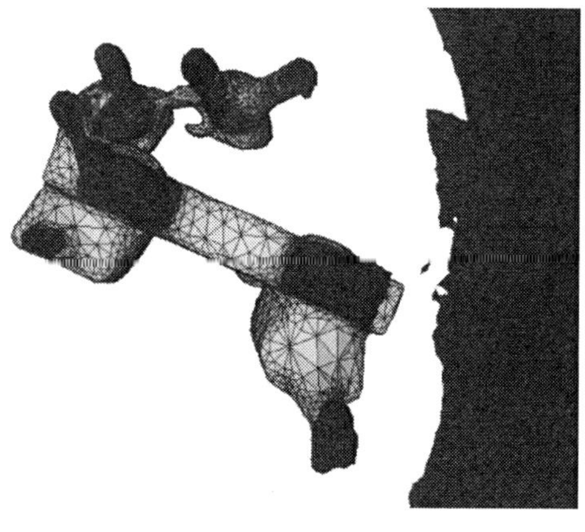

Figure 3. Polygon model of the statues introduced in Figure 1. By detecting an enclosed hollow, our approach determines the statues upright position. Implicitly, the base level is found. A threshold is necessary to identify an unleveled base of the statue (right).

C. Observations

From the data collected during monitoring in the setting we describe above, we observed that 29 subjects rotated the 3D object into the bird's perspective. In this view, they used the volume function and placed the square volume around the foundation of the figure in the 3D object. After placing the volume, 24 subjects rotated the view around the object multiple times. 17 subjects returned to the bird's perspective and changed the volume selection. The other 5 subjects continued straight away. Monitoring data reveals that the subjects used a mean of 5 (min: 4; max: 12) rotating interactions, in order to rotate the object into the bird's perspective.

Placing the object in an upright position was achieved by 26 subjects. Tracking data reveals that they rotated the object multiple times. 22 subjects oriented at first and rotated the figure until it was placed correctly on the horizontal layer. The other 4 subjects rotated the figure multiple times without any obvious pattern. From the 22 subjects, 19 continued by using the orientation tool to point at the figures' front and saved the front-facing figure as default view for the 3D objects. The other 3 subjects were not able to complete the task successfully. Monitoring data reveals that the 19 successful subjects used a mean of 8 (min: 2; max: 14) rotating interactions, in order to rotate the object into the front facing view.

For an experienced user, with a desktop system, the interaction of rotating and cutting takes around 30s. The successful subjects completed the task in a median time of 116s (min: 29s; max: 755s). From those using a touch-screen, the median was slightly higher with 201s. This time can potentially be saved using an auto-enhance process running in the background.

D. Findings

From the observations, we derive the following algorithm, described here in functional pseudo-code.

rotateToBirdsView();
findBaseContours();
cutObject();
rotateUpright();

The bird's view plays a vital role in the process to remove unwanted surroundings. Rotating an object to the bird's perspective can be achieved by rotating the object until the maximum depth of an enclosed hollow is found. This enclosed hollow is formed by the figure, which's surface forms the hull of the enclosed hollow (see Figure 3). Flipping the camera coordinates to the opposite position gives the bird's view. From our lab experiments we derive that only 3 out of 51 3D objects cannot be rotated using this heuristic, as the unwanted surroundings in 49 reconstructed 3D objects form layers and surfaces without enclosed hollows.

From the bird's perspective, the subjects recognized the contours of the figure inside the 3D object and consequently placed the volume around the contours. For an automated algorithm, we can derive that from each point of the volumes base drawn around the contours of that figure, a clipping search for polygons directed inwards along the x- and y-axis yields a value, which represents the distance of that point on the volume's base to the contours of the figure. As the base of a figure in 51 reconstructed objects is never totally flat, a threshold to detect the contours of the figures base is necessary to take into account. The result of this step of the algorithm is the placement of a volume from the direction of the bird's perspective camera on to the base of the volume. As the volume's projection across the entire object at intersects with the ground level, the figure is assumed to be standing on, a check for orthogonality verifies whether the object's contours for the volume's base was detected.

In the next step, the 3D object is cut according to the given volume. This method is part of 3DEdit and already implemented using Blender [16] to perform all necessary operations on the 3D object itself. Figure 4 illustrates the ideal result.

In the next step, upright rotation is achieved by transforming the 3D object according to its horizontal base and the orthogonal camera view.

In the last step, our observations yield many patterns of user interaction on order to find the face view of the 3D object. However, although 19 subjects were successful in reorienting the 3D object, we were not able to derive a general pattern an algorithm can perform without any user interaction in an ambient context. In this final step, it is again not possible to use approaches of our related work, as, e.g., the figures base is not closed. In a previous step, we exploited these characteristics of the figure in order to find its bird's view. Apart from the figure's base, the related work stops at rotating a figure upright and terminates in any upright position. In an initial approach, we will consider means of facial recognition, in order to find the front view of a certain class of 3D objects. Another approach would be to calculate different possibilities as preview options and offer the user a choice between the most likely options. When selected, the calculations are performed automatically.

This approach is supposed to work on figures or statues or objects of equivalent characteristics. For any other type of object characteristics, other means of automation still need to be evaluated.

Figure 4. Ideal result. This manually edited sculpture serves as reference for our approach to auto-enhance 3D object enhancement.

VI. Summary and Outlook

Through NEMO, semantic photographic media created by students using their smartphones in mobile context is automatically converted into 3D objects for further use in Ambient Learning Spaces and especially the ALS mobile apps. Although we developed a solution to enhance these automatically created 3D objects in only two steps of cutting and rotating using 3DEdit, in order to remove artefacts or cut out a certain part of a 3D object, this process still requires user interaction.

In this contribution, we present our initial approach to automate the process of enhancing 3D objects in the ambient context of our scenario. Using our frontend editor 3DEdit, we illustrate how we use observations from user interactions to get valuable data in order to define a first approach to automate the process of enhancing 3D objects from 3D object reconstruction. In our ongoing work of our research project, we focus on the implementation and validation of our algorithm.

It is our hypothesis that formal, non-formal, and informal learning through ALS media in a digitally enriched learning space fosters cognitive skills and knowledge in the communicative environment [4] of ALS. We are going to evaluate this in more detail in within schools as well as in museums. Therefore, 3D objects play a vital role in our research. We plan to evaluate their values in a digitally enriched learning environment, e.g., with our school and museum project partners.

For our museum project partners, we have developed scenarios integrating 3D objects into exhibitions with special focus on the autonomous use inside the museums. In this context, the curators experience in the selection process of 3D objects to augment an exhibition can be enhanced with 3DEdit. Therefore, 3DEdit offers a solution to enable curators to edit 3D objects from any source [17]. In our further work, we are going to evaluate the curators' user experiences using our ALS systems.

For any ALS application of the research project, among other features, NEMO provides persistent storage of semantically Enriched Media. The ALS applications are featuring the creation, presentation, use and interaction with such Enriched Media. Together with our project partners, two schools and two museums located in the Hanseatic City of Luebeck, Germany, the use of these applications together with NEMO in context of mobile and ambient learning is currently being further evaluated.

Acknowledgment

We develop NEMO and ALS applications in the ongoing research project "Ambient Learning Spaces" supported by the German Research Foundation (Deutsche Forschungsgemeinschaft, DFG). We also thank our school and museum project partners for their kind support.

References

[1] D. Bouck-Standen et al., "Reconstruction and Web-based Editing of 3D Objects from Photo and Video Footage for Ambient Learning Spaces," *Int. J. Adv. Intell. Syst.*, vol. 11, IARIA, pp. 94-108, 2018.

[2] T. Winkler, F. Scharf, C. Hahn, and M. Herczeg, "Ambient Learning Spaces," *Educ. a Technol. World Commun. Curr. Emerg. Res. Technol. Efforts*, pp. 56-67, 2011.

[3] K. Persefoni and A. Tsinakos, "Use of augmented reality in terms of creativity in school learning," *CEUR Workshop Proc.*, vol. 1450, *September*, pp. 45-53, 2015.

[4] T. Winkler, D. Bouck-Standen, M. Ide, A. Ohlei, and M. Herczeg, "InteractiveWall 3.1 - Formal and Non-Formal Learning at School with Web-3.0-based Technology in Front of Large Multi-touch Screens," in *EdMedia: World Conf. on Educational Media and Techn.*, Washington, DC: AACE, *Outstanding Paper Award*, pp. 1317-1326, 2017.

[5] D. Bouck-Standen, "Construction of an API connecting the Network Environment for Multimedia Objects with Ambient Learning Spaces," Master Thesis, Lübeck, Germany, 2016, doi: 10.13140/RG.2.2.12155.00804.

[6] D. Bouck-Standen, A. Ohlei, V. Daibert, T. Winkler, and M. Herczeg, "NEMO Converter 3D: Reconstruction of 3D Objects from Photo and Video Footage for Ambient Learning Spaces," in *AMBIENT 2017 - Best Paper Award; The Seventh Int. Conf. on Ambient Computing, Applications, Services and Technologies*, IARIA, pp. 6-12, 2017.

[7] A. Ohlei, D. Bouck-Standen, T. Winkler, and M. Herczeg, "InfoGrid: Acceptance and Usability of Augmented Reality for Mobiles in Real Museum Context (In Press)," *Mensch und Comput. 2018 - Work.*, pp. 1-8, 2018.

[8] J. H. and O. L. T. Berners-Lee, "The Semantic Web," in *Scientific American*, pp. 30-37, 2001.

[9] F. Nack, "The future in digital media computing is meta," *IEEE Multimed.*, vol. 11, no. 2, pp. 10-13, 2004.

[10] P. Bouquet and A. Molinari, "A New Approach to the Use of Semantic Technologies in E-Learning Platforms," *Int. J. Adv. Corp. Learn.*, vol. 9, p. 5, 2016.

[11] M. Dougiamas and P. Taylor, "Moodle: Using Learning Communities to Create an Open Source Course Management System," *Research.Moodle.Net*, January, pp. 1-16, 2003.

[12] R. Arnold, "How to Teach without Instructing: 29 Smart Rules for Educators," *Rowman & Littlefield*, Lanham, 2015.

[13] H. Fu, D. Cohen-Or, G. Dror, and A. Sheffer, "Upright orientation of man-made objects," *ACM SIGGRAPH 2008 Pap. - SIGGRAPH '08*, pp. 1-7, 2008.

[14] Y. Jin, Q. Wu, and L. Liu, "Unsupervised upright orientation of man-made models," *Graph. Models*, vol. 74, no. 4, pp. 99-108, 2012.

[15] B. Jiang, M. Zeng, and X. Liu, "An upright orientation detection algorithm for 3D man-made objects based on shape properties," *Journal Comput. Des. Comput. Graph.*, vol. 25, pp. 1099-1106, 2013.

[16] Blender. [Online]. Accessed 27 July 2018. Available: https://www.blender.org

[17] A. Ohlei, D. Bouck-Standen, T. Winkler, and M. Herczeg, "InfoGrid: An Approach for Curators to Digitally Enrich their Exhibitions," *Mensch u. Comput. 2018 - Work.*, pp. 345-352, 2018.

MCA Driven Interaction Interfacing

Daniela Elisabeth Ströckl
Institute of Applied Research on Aging
Carinthia University of Applied Sciences
Klagenfurt, Austria
e-mail: d.stroeckl@fh-kaernten.at

Heinrich C. Mayr
Institute of Applied Informatics
Alpen-Adria-Universität
Klagenfurt, Austria
e-mail: Heinrich.Mayr@aau.at

Abstract— **Assistive technologies can help older people stay at home longer and more independently. Like any other user group, seniors have specific profiles and demands that are to be considered when designing such technologies. This paper presents an approach to multimodal user interface design and development based on the Model-Centered Architecture paradigm. The research is part of the Human Behavior Monitoring and Support (HBMS) project that aims at providing a comprehensive assistive system. The approach should enable assistive systems to be flexibly adapted to any user needs with regard to interaction and corresponding end devices.**

Keywords-Model-Centered Architecture; Conceptual Modelling; Smart Home; Active & Assisted Living; AAL; Assistance System; Activities of Daily Living; ADLs.

I. Introduction

In a technology-driven approach, the use of devices such as smartphones, tablet computers or household appliances is gradually becoming a standard in everyday life. However, elderly people or people with impairments have trouble to interact with such devices depending on their individual disabilities. Therefore, several researchers are working on multimodal development strategies to facilitate the interaction between humans and systems.

Complex interactions are a challenge for users and developers. In particular, a system should allow the user to communicate in a convenient and natural way in any usage situation. Therefore, a system should be aware of the context, learn, and behave according to the particular user. Examples for related work dealing with multimodal human-system interactions are: models for multimodal interaction by Dausend et al. [1], multimodal interaction in smart environments by Blumendorf [2], or Conceptual Modeling of Interactions by Aquino et al. [3].

This paper presents an approach that exploits the Model Centered Architecture (MCA) paradigm for designing and developing multimodal interfaces of assistive systems in the context of Active and Assisted Living (AAL). The aspects communicated via such interface are conceptualized in a meta-model that, in turn, forms the basis of a Domain Specific Modeling Language (DSML). Based on this, interface specifications for any device and content consist in models created using that DSML. The system should be flexible enough to select from a group of different interactive media and devices one suitable for each person to help with activities at home. We will illustrate this approach by means of an interface specification for the Human Behavior Monitoring and Support (HBMS) system [4].

The paper's structure is as follows: Section II outlines the main aspects of MCA. Section III shortly describes the HBMS system. In Section IV, we sketch the scenario, which we will use for illustrating our approach. In Section V, we present the most important concepts of the metamodel for the multimodal interface specification we have developed and a model instantiated from this metamodel. Section VI discusses an excerpt from a concrete interface description. The paper closes with an outlook on future work.

II. Model Centered Architecture

MCA focusses on models and their meta-models in any development step of software systems. For example, the functionality as well as all interfaces of a system are specified as conceptual models using appropriate Domain Specific modeling Languages (DSMLs) for that purpose. Consequently, all system components are seen as model handlers in the sense of model consumers and/or producers [5].

MCA exploits the model hierarchy as defined in the Meta Object Facility (MOF) [6]: Using a standard meta-meta-model with a pre-defined notation on the M3 level, we determine the meta-models (and for representational purposes the DSMLs) [7] for the various interfaces and the application domain on the M2 (meta-model) level. The M1 level models are extensions of these meta-models and determine a particular system application. The extensions of these models on the M0 level then represent the concrete processes and data of the running system. For example, every input/output device as well as any functional system module deals with or produces extensions of one or more M1 models [8].

III. Example Application Environment: HBMS

The aim of the HBMS system is to provide elderly people with unobtrusive support in their everyday activities. It uses the output of Human Activity Recognition (HAR) systems [9] to learn a user's strategies for mastering his or her home activities, establishes a Human Cognitive Model (HCM), which then is exploited when situations are detected in which the user needs support [4]. In the best case, a HBMS system instance is set up in a user's environment before dementia processes interfere with the learning process

[10]. The development strategy of the HBMS system strictly follows the MCA paradigm.

The system consists of several components, among which we list:

- HCM-L Modeling Tool: supports the Human Cognitive Modeling Language (HCM-L), a DSML defined for establishing human cognitive models, as mentioned before. The tool has been generated using the ADOxx meta-modeling framework [11].
- HBMS Kernel, consisting of
  - Observation Engine: investigates the behaviour and context of the end user through coupled HAR systems in order to identify her/his goals and actions to achieve these goals.
  - Behavior Engine: evaluates the observed behavior and context, as well as a database of former support cases, and decides on how to proceed according to the HCM; in parallel, new activities and situations are learned.
  - Support Engine: provides the end user with situational support information via the human-system interface.
- HBMS Database: A triple store containing all data: HCM, models and meta-models, domain ontology, case base, and a situational cache describing the current situation [4].

IV. Human-System Interaction: Interfaces & Devices

Within this section, we sketch a scenario we selected for a proof of concept, the input/output devices used in each case, and the DSML for specifying the interfaces for these devices.

The scenario "Morning Routine" consists of several sub-scenarios: brushing teeth, washing face, washing hands, comp hair and apply a cream on face. All these sub-scenarios are feasible in different sequences during the morning routine. The user of the assistive system should get support in this routine whenever she/he needs, for example when searching items like the toothbrush, forgetting to put toothpaste on the brush, and so forth [12].

For this scenario, suitable devices are a boundary microphone for user commands, a mini-beamer for showing short videos, a lightbulb for warnings and, possibly, a tablet computer to show mixed content like text, pictures and videos [12]. Figure 1 shows a use case interaction diagram 2.0 (UC-UI Diagram 2.0) describing the interaction in the "washing face" sub-scenario [13].

V. Meta-Model and DSML for Interface Specification

This section presents the specification of our multimodal interface on all MOF levels excluding level 3 for which we choose a self-explanatory standard notation (as used in Figure 2 for the meta-model specification).

The symbols in the left upper corner of the meta-model represent the notation of the corresponding DSML concepts used when creating models on M1. The main concepts are "Interaction Mode" for capturing the various kinds of information representation, and "Interaction Entity" for capturing the interaction units including user input.

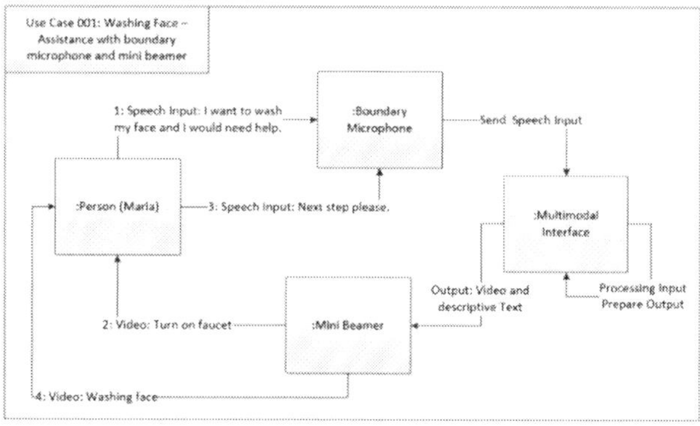

Figure 1. UC-UI Diagram 2.0 for the scenario "Washing Face"

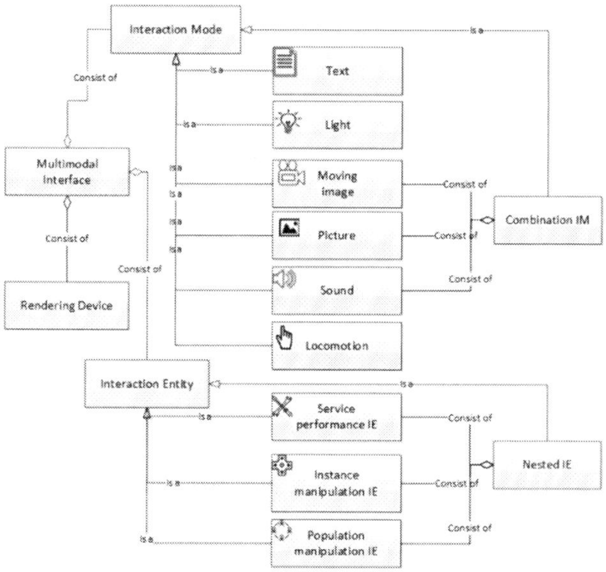

Figure 2. Meta-model (simplified) for the HBMS multimodal human-system interaction

The concepts "Combination IM" and "Nested IE" are introduced to cover situations where multiple modes are combined or user interactions consist of multiple partial interactions. "Rendering device" captures, for a given interaction mode, the device(s) used. For reasons of simplicity and also due to the space limit we omitted in Figure 2 the M2 concept "Attribute" as well as the concept "Relation" (e.g., for describing the relationships between Interaction Modes and Interaction Entities, and between Interaction Entity and Rendering Device).

Figure 3 shows an instantiation of the meta-model given in Figure 2 on level M1. It describes the modes and units that are relevant for the morning routine scenario. Note that this is still an abstraction (a conceptual model), which could be appropriate also for describing the "interfaces" for other activities to be supported.

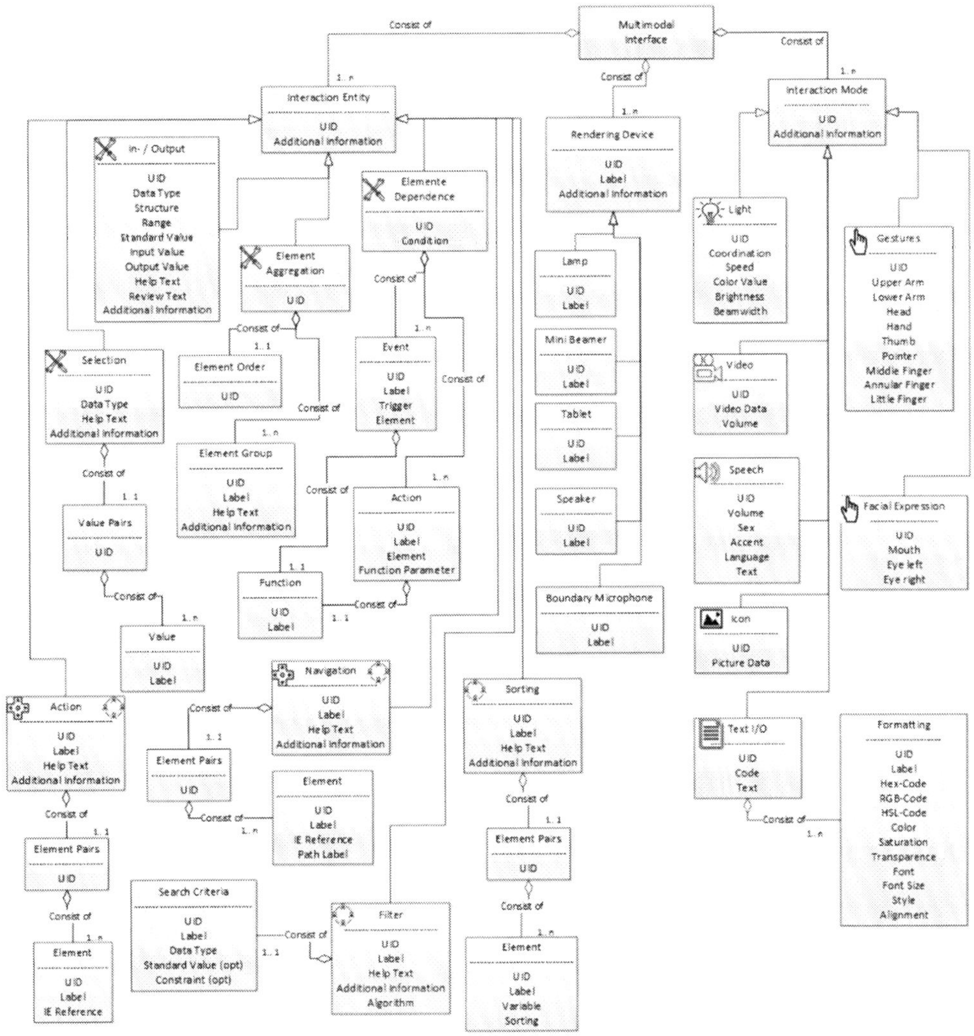

Figure 3. Example of a model (M1)

Consequently, the concrete devices, interaction units and their relationships are instantiated on level M0. We omitted, again for simplicity, the model details of the rendering devices.

The advantage of this approach is that this data can largely be generated on the basis of the M0 models if the corresponding units (text fragments, video clips, etc.) are available in a database. In addition, a standard module (in the case of the HBMS system, the support module) can then control any type of modeled interaction.

VI. Representation on Level M0

In order to show the "code" that results on level M0 on the basis of such models, we give below an excerpt from this code. It describes the possible interactions during a "washing face" action (as part of the "morning routine" activity). In particular, the devices "boundary microphone" and "mini beamer" are addressed.

All these tasks provide the possibility to show a short video about how to process. While the user finished the task, a "finished" speech input will be recorded with the boundary microphone and this leads to the next introduction video.

In this code (Figure 4), fictional variables are chosen for all the elements represented in the M0 level models.

```
<Multimodal Interface>
    <Rendering Device>
        <Mini beamer UID="1"; label="Output device mini-beamer";/>
        <Boundary Microphone UID="2"; label="audio record with a
        boundary microphone";/>
    </ Rendering Device >
    <Interaction Mode>
        <Speech UID="1"; Volume="74dB"; Sex="NULL";
        Accent="NULL"; Language="English"; Text="NULL";/>
    </Interaction Mode>
    <Interaction Entity>
        <Input UID="1"; Data Type="MP3"; Structure="NULL";
        Range="NULL"; Standard Value="NULL"; Input Value="I want
        to wash my face and I would need help."; Output
```

```
    Value="NULL"; Help Text="NULL"; Review Text="NULL";
    Additional Information="NULL"; />
    <Action UID="1"; Label="Speech recognition with grammer";
    Help Text="NULL"; Additional Information="Instruction will be
    extracted out of speech input";/>
            <Elements UID="1"; />
            <Element UID="1"; Label="Fragment out of
            speech recognition"; IE Reference="Input 001"; />
    <Action UID="2"; Label="Play video Wash face"; Help
    Text="NULL"; Additional Information="Starting assistance for
    washing the face"; />
            <Elements UID="2"; />
            <Element UID="2"; Label="Loading
            turn_on_faucet.mp4"; IE Reference="Input 001"; />
  </Interaction Entity>
  <Interaction Mode>
    <Video UID="1"; Video Data="turn_on_faucet.mp4";
    Volume="80dB"; />
    <Description UID="01"; Code="UTF-8"; Text="Before you can
    wash your face you have to turn on the faucet."; />
        <Format UID="1"; Label="Video description"; HEX-
        Code="#000000"; RGB-Code="0, 0, 0"; HSL-Code="0,
        0%, 0%"; Color="Schwarz"; Saturation="100%";
        Transparence="0%"; Font Type="Verdana"; Font
        Size="15pt"; Stile="San Serif"; Alignment="left"; />
    <Speech UID="2"; Volume="75dB"; Sex="NULL";
    Accent="NULL"; Language="NULL"; Text="NULL"; />
  </Interaction Mode>
  <Interaction Entity>
    <Input UID="2"; Data Type="MP3"; Structure="NULL";
    Range="NULL"; Standard Value="NULL"; Input
    Value="What's next??"; Output Value="NULL"; Help
    Text="NULL"; Review Text="NULL"; Additional
    Information="NULL"; />
    <Element Dependence UID="1"; Condition="Video 2 after
    Video 1"; />
    <Event UID="1"; Label="Play Video 2 after Video 1";
    Trigger="Speech input"; Element="speechinput.mp3"; />
            </Function UID="1"; Label="Turn of Video 1"; />
    <Action UID="3"; Label="Play wash_face.mp4";
    Element="Input 02"; Function Parameter="wash_face.mp4"; />
            <Function UID="02"; Label ="Start video 2"; />
    ...
</ Multimodal Interface >
```

Figure 4. Code example referring to the scenario "Washing face"

Clearly, after having formally defined a comprehensive representation language, such code may be generated automatically, e.g., based on the framework we have developed in the context of HBMS for linking activity recognition systems to the HBMS system. In particular, we can reuse a parser exploiting the ANTLR framework to generate code fragments out of internal data representations that are stored as OWL individuals [14].

VII. CONCLUSION

This paper explained the current state of work regarding our metamodel for specifying multimodel interfaces for ambient systems that support people in a smart home. The next step will be integrating this approach into the HBMS environment, and providing the models for all kinds of interactions to be supported. These will be refinements of the model shown in Figure 3 by following the multilevel modeling approach, as presented in [15]. Then, tests will be carried out in a lab situation by user experiments. This means that, besides functional testing, seniors will also test the system: with a "think aloud method" they will give feedback to improve the approach.

REFERENCES

[1] M. Dausend and M. Poguntke, "Executable UML models of multimodal interaction applications." In: Ziegler, J. (eds), i-com: Vol. 10, No. 3. München: Oldenbourg Wissenschaftsverlag GmbH. 2011. pp. 33-39.

[2] D. Roscher, M. Blumendorf, and S. Albayrak, "A meta user interface to control multimodal interaction in smart environments." IUI '09 Proceedings of the 14th international conference on Intelligent user interfaces, 2019, Florida. ISBN: 978-1-60558-168-2

[3] N. Aquino, J. Vanderdonckt, J. Panach, and O. Pastor, "Conceptual Modelling of Interaction", Springer. D.W. Embley and B. Thalheim (eds), Handbook of Conceptual Modeling. Springer, 2011, DOI: 10.1007/978-3-642-15865-0

[4] J. Michael, et al.: "The HBMS Story." In: Enterprise Modelling and Information Systems Architectures – International Journal of Conceptual Modeling, Vol. 13, 2018, pp. 345-370.

[5] H. C. Mayr, J. Michael, S. Ranasinghe, V. Shekhovtsov, and C. Steinberger, "Model Centered Architecture". Cabot et al. (eds.), Conceptual Modeling Perspectives. Springer International Publishing. 2017.

[6] Object Management Group (OMG) OMG Meta Object Facility (MOF) Core Specification Version 2.5.1., 2016, [Accessed: June 2018]

[7] S. Kelly, and J. Tolvanen, "Domain-Specific Modeling: Enabling Full Code Generation." Wiley, 2008, IEEE. ISBN: 978-0-47003-666-2

[8] J. Alvarez, A. Evans, and P. Sammut, "Mapping between Levels in the Metamodel Architecture." In: Gogola M.. Kobryn C. (eds.): UML 2001 – The Unified Modeling Language: Modeling Languages, Concepts and Tools. Springer, Berlin, 2001.

[9] S. Ranasinghe, F. Al Machot, and H. C. Mayr, "A Review on Applications of Activity Recognition Systems with Regard to Performance and Evaluation." Int. Journal of Distributed Sensor Networks, 12(8), 2016. DOI: 10.1177/1550147716665520

[10] H. C. Mayr, "HBMS Research Topics". In: HBMS – Human Behavior Monitoring and Support. Accessed: June 2018. http://hbms-ainf.aau.at/en/hbms-research-topics.html

[11] M. Esperguel, and S. Sepulveda, "Feature modeling tool: a proposal using ADOxx technology." Computing Conference (CLEI), 2016 XLII Latin American, Chile. 2017, ISBN: 978-1-5090-1634-1

[12] D. E. Ströckl, "Scenario based Development Approach towards a Multi-modal Interface Presentation Meta-model." Proceedings Smarter Lives '18, 2018, Innsbruck.

[13] D. E. Ströckl, D. Krainer, and E. Oberrauner, „Improving Interdisciplinary Communication – Use Case Focused User Interaction Diagram 2.0." Ambient '18, 2018, in press.

[14] V. Shekhovtsov et al., "Domain Specific Models as System Links." Advances in Conceptual Modeling, Springer, LNCS Vol 11158, pp. 330-341, 2018.

[15] U. Frank, "Multilevel Modeling. Business & Information Systems Engineering," Vol.5, 2014.

SMILA: Design and Evaluation of a Smart Mirror for Monitoring Health

Karl Kreiner
Center for Health and Bioresources
AIT Austrian Institute of Technology GmbH
Graz, Austria
e-mail: karl.kreiner@ait.ac.at

Christian Löw
Research Group Cooperative Systems (COSY)
University of Vienna
Vienna, Austria
e-mail: christian.loew@univie.ac.at

Svenja Schröder
Research Group Cooperative Systems (COSY)
University of Vienna
Vienna, Austria
e-mail: svenja.schroeder@univie.ac.at

Markus Falgenhauer
Center for Health and Bioresources
AIT Austrian Institute of Technology GmbH
Graz, Austria
e-mail: markus.falgenhauer@ait.ac.at

Kristina Reiter
Center for Health and Bioresources
AIT Austrian Institute of Technology GmbH
Graz, Austria
e-mail: kristina.reiter@ait.ac.at

Kurt Edegger
Center for Health and Bioresources
AIT Austrian Institute of Technology GmbH
Graz, Austria
e-mail: kurt.edegger@ait.ac.at

Abstract— **Chronic diseases among elderly people have an increasing impact on healthcare systems. Telehealth interventions using smart phones and low-cost sensors have been shown to potentially increase quality of life and reduce re-hospitalization rates. While usage of Internet and smart phones is generally increasing in elderly people, there is still a digital divide between younger and older users making usability a key aspect of telehealth intervention design. In this work, we introduce SMILA, an interactive, voice-controlled smart mirror supporting elderly people in self-monitoring of parameters relevant to chronic heart failure. We present the design, construction, user identification using wrist-bands and linkage of the mirror to a telehealth service based on the Internet of Things mediation framework *symbIoTe*. Finally, we present initial results from a pilot study evaluating user acceptance and usability.**

Keywords- smart mirror; telehealth; human-computer interaction; smart home; Internet of Things.

I. Introduction

The economic policy committee estimated that in 2050, one in three Europeans will be older than 65 years [1], with the process of aging being influenced by various factors, such as employment, education lifestyle and presence or absence of chronic diseases. Especially cardiovascular diseases have a huge impact on quality of life and hospitalization rates. The rise of smartphones and low-cost sensors has led to new health interventions referred to as telehealth, allowing patients to track health parameters at home using a smartphone, feeding this data into health data centers for inspection by health professionals. Telehealth interventions have shown to reduce hospitalization rates [2] and - by promoting self-management knowledge and skills - support preventative approaches that are key to managing chronic disease [3].

While the use of Information and Communication Technologies (ICT) is generally increasing in elderly people, it has been shown that there is a digital divide between young and elderly people when it comes to ICT usage, especially in elderly people with low education and income, as well as physical frailty status being directly related to ICT usage [4].

Aside from smartphones, the last decade saw a rise of smart objects commonly referred to as Internet of Things (IoT) especially in the area of health. Examples include fitness wristbands measuring heart rate, sleep duration and quality and daily activity. From a technical perspective, these devices are usually tied to vendor-specific IoT platforms leading to a large fragmentation of the IT landscape. The EU-funded project symbIoTe (symbiosis of smart objects) [5] seeks to implement a mediation framework between these platforms providing application developers with unified interfaces across different IoT platforms on various levels, such as hardware and software and the network layer.

Against the backlight of these developments, the objective of our work is to investigate how an unobtrusive telehealth intervention in the area of cardiovascular disease can be designed and built on top of the symbIoTe mediation framework.

We introduce Smart Mirror Integrated Living Assistant (SMILA), an interactive smart mirror for assisting elderly people with daily measurements of physiological parameters relevant for the treatment of cardiovascular diseases.

"Smart mirrors" are devices mounted to the background of a semi-transparent mirror in order to augment the reflective surface of the mirror with digital information.

The use of smart mirrors in a health context is interesting as people use a mirror on a daily basis. The use of smart mirrors in the context of health has been investigated in a number of scenarios: "Fit Mirror" [6], a smart mirror using gesture control to provide physical exercises to elderly people, "Wize Mirror" [7] using 3D optical sensors, multispectral cameras and gas detection sensors to derive a wellbeing Index and a non-contact health monitoring system [8] analyses facial expressions, posture and voice changes.

The contribution of our work to this field is two-fold: (1) we merge the concepts of telehealth interventions in the area of cardiovascular disease with the smart mirror concept and (2) we aim to investigate end-user acceptance with two stakeholder groups (a) eldery people and (b) young people in order to explore differences in user interaction between these two groups.

The rest of this paper is organized as follows: First, we describe the design of the interactive mirror. Second, we describe how the end-user evaluation design has been setup. Third, we describe the overall interaction workflow and discuss results from an initial user evaluation.

II. METHODS

A. *Smart mirror*

SMILA was constructed of a wooden frame (40x30x4 cm, gross weight 2,5kg) housing the semi-transparent mirror hiding a Samsung Galaxy Tab A 10.1 Android tablet. The idea for constructing the smart mirror from scratch and not taking a commercially available product was primarily economically driven. By using off the shelf materials and simple constructions, the total costs for one smart mirror could be held below 300€.

In idle mode, the mirror displays the current time and the weather situation at its current location. We decided against showing more information for several reasons: (1) to prevent information overload and to only provide context-relevant information and (2) to keep battery and bandwidth usage low.

B. *Sensors and user-recognition*

As we chose the area of cardiovascular diseases, a number of vital parameters are interesting facing the telehealth perspective: regular measurements of heart rate, blood pressure, body weight and daily activity are relevant to the therapy in order to assess effectiveness, as well as to detect any deterioration in a person's health status. For initial evaluation, we chose connecting the smart mirror to a Bluetooth-enabled scale for two reasons. (1) a scale is most likely to be found in bathrooms and (2) a sudden increase in weight is an indicator for hospitalization [9]. Moreover, SMILA uses voice input to collect information on personal well-being using Google's Cloud Speech Application Programming Interface (API).

Another important aspect is user identification, as most likely many people are living in a two-person household. We considered several options for user identification: (1) identification and authorization by a separate device using PIN codes once the device is close to the mirror (2) facial recognition and (3) wearable Bluetooth low energy beacons for identification.

Bluetooth Low Energy (BLE) beacons are devices transmitting signals containing their ID along with other technical information on a regular interval. Devices such as smartphones or tablets can identify these radio signals within a limited range and apps can react to the presence of such beacons. We favored this approach especially to biometric identification as it is (1) more privacy-preserving and (2) BLE beacons can be exchanged by fitness wristbands, thus combining identification with reading further health measurements. BLE beacons have been used in various scenarios, most prominently in eCommerce settings offering consumers guide within shops. For our initial evaluation, we decided to use wristband type beacons or devices that can be attached to a keychain (D15 UFO Bluetooth). The latter can be incorporated in a necklace as well.

SMILA is connected to the KIOLA telehealth platform, a data collection framework and therapy management system for various chronic diseases [10]. Weight measurements and personal well-being are collected through SMILA and then transmitted to KIOLA. To provide interoperability to other platforms (e.g., consumer health platforms), data transmission and retrieval is handled through the symbIoTe mediation framework using standardized RESTful interfaces.

C. *End-user evaluation design*

End-user evaluation of SMILA was conducted at the COSY Living Lab at the University of Vienna, a multi-purpose user study laboratory equipped with furnishing and technical set-up to support a home-like test-setting that is observable through semi-transparent windows and audio-visual equipment. We designed a lab-evaluation concept that aims at collecting overall usability feedback to the SMILA prototype as well as inquiring the participant's own experience with health monitoring tasks and relating the SMILA concept to it. We conducted semi-structured interviews [11] that establish such personal experience regarding medical monitoring and self-management with chronic disease as well as regarding technology usage in this context and generally, in order to answer the research question: *Can SMILA support the way the participants manage self-monitoring tasks with chronic conditions?* This was followed by observation of participants using SMILA in the Living Lab while they complete a pre-defined task of monitoring their weight and overall well-being as well as a concluding survey on experience and usability of the smart mirror's audio-visual interface and interaction, utilizing the System Usability Scale (SUS) [12].

The evaluation was carried out in two phases: first, the prototype was tested with university students to gain initial feedback and test feasibility of the system. Second, the prototype was tested following the same schema with elderly people.

III. RESULTS

A. *Overall workflow*

The end-user wears a BLE-enabled wristband and enters the bathroom. In idle mode, SMILA constantly scans for BLE signals and reads the ID of recognized beacons. Using this ID it queries the symbIoTe mediation framework, receives an access URL for the KIOLA tele-health platform and receives personal information on the user resulting in an acoustic personal greeting. It then asks the end-user to step on the scale performing the measurement (see Figure 1). While standing on the scale, SMILA displays the current weight (as seen in Figure 2) on the display. Once the measurement is taken, SMILA finishes asking for the personal wellbeing with the-end-user answering using voice-input. Finally, using the ID of the scale, SMILA queries the symbIoTe mediation platform for an end-point and transmits the data to the KIOLA telehealth platform. The whole process is guided through voice output.

Figure 1. From left to right: (1) Living lab evaluation scenario; (2) SMILA and (3) user interacting with the device

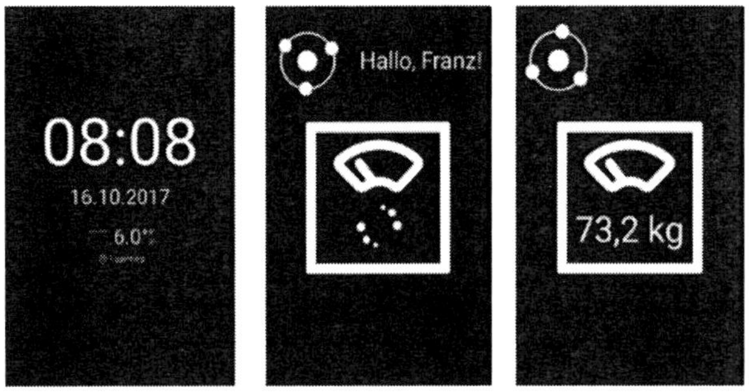

Figure 2. From left to right: (1) mirror idle – showing time and temperature; (2) greeting specific user and guiding through the workflow; (3) SMILA showing the result of a weight measurement

B. *Evaluation results*

The user evaluation was conducted in two phases with 18 participants providing initial insights on the technical feasibility and basic usability of the SMILA prototype. Evaluation was conducted in two groups with group A consisting of 11 participants (4 female / 7 male; 18-35), all students of computer science. Group B consisted of 7 participants (6 male / 1 female; 60-69 years old). During the test, the participants had to follow SMILA's vocal instructions of stepping on the scale and getting their weight, as well as entering their current state of being via voice input. 16 out of 18 tests were completed successfully. Personal well-being has been correctly translated into text in 9 out of 10 cases with the speech recognition API providing a confidence score (a score between 0 and 1) of 0.83 (±0.13) on average. Average length of inputs was 3.81 (±2.72) words.

When asked if users could picture themselves using the device at home, 10 answered with yes, 4 with maybe and 4 could not think of using the device at home.

IV. DISCUSSION

Interviews revealed potential usability improvements, such as a perceived lag between stepping in front of the mirror and being identified, as well as uncertainty when voice input was possible. Moreover, participants complained about the "robotic voice" as provided by voice output. Feedback on design included the incorporation of the bracelet into jewelry (e.g. a brooch) and both groups suggested face recognition or voice recognition as alternative form of user recognition though both groups raised privacy issues. When asked for additional usage scenarios for the mirror, elderly people named (a) support in management tasks (blood pressure measurements), assistance with medication intake and medication reminders, as well as support of scheduling appointments with physicians. In terms of the overall interactional quality, elderly participants consistently voiced their preference for such technology to have a "companion-like" quality they can have a trusted relationship with, rather than a tool for easy communication with medical and care professionals.

University students named benefits in supporting adherence to fitness goals.

V. CONCLUSION AND FUTURE WORK

We presented a smart mirror for self-monitoring of health parameters relevant to cardiovascular therapy. User identification using BLE-wristbands is feasible and initial evaluations showed that the method is reliable, though a higher responsiveness of the system is required. Moreover, using BLE wristbands has security implications that need to be addressed in further research. Using voice recognition for recording personal well-being proved to be sufficiently accurate in a controlled environment.

Next steps include the extension of workflow to include smart watches as mode of user recognition and the inclusion of fitness data for display on the mirror. This setting will be tested in another trial, where users can test the device over the period of one week.

ACKNOWLEDGMENTS

This work is supported by the symbIoTe project, which has received funding from the European Union's Horizon 2020 research and innovation program under grant agreement No 688156.

REFERENCES

[1] Economic Policy Committee. *Impact of ageing populations on public spending on pensions, health and long-term care, education and unemployment benefits for the elderly.* [Online]. Available from: https://europa.eu/epc/, 2018.10.29

[2] S. Scalvini et al., "Effect of home-based telecardiology on chronic heart failure: costs and outcomes." Journal of telemedicine and telecare vol. 11, pp. 16-18, 2005.

[3] M. Solomon, S.L. Wagner, and J. Goes, "Effects of a Web-based intervention for adults with chronic conditions on patient activation: online randomized controlled trial." Journal of medical Internet research vol. 14, 2012.

[4] N.S. Keränen, M. Kangas, M. Immonen, H. Similä, H. Enwald, R. Korpelainen, et al., "Use of information and communication technologies among older people with and without frailty: a population-based survey." Journal of medical Internet research vol. 19, 2017.

[5] M. Jacoby, A. Antonić, K. Kreiner, R. Lapacz, and J. Pielorz, "Semantic Interoperability as Key to IoT Platform Federation." International Workshop on Interoperability and Open-Source Solutions. Springer, Cham, 2016, pp. 3-19.

[6] D. Besserer, J. Bäurle, A. Nikic, F. Honold, F. Schüssel, and M. Weber, "Fitmirror: a smart mirror for positive affect in everyday user morning routines." Proceedings of the Workshop on Multimodal Analyses enabling Artificial Agents in Human-Machine Interaction. ACM, pp. 48-55, 2016.

[7] S. Colantonio et al., "A smart mirror to promote a healthy lifestyle." Biosystems Engineering vol. 138, pp. 33-43, 2015.

[8] N. Yang, X. Zhao and H. Zhang, "A non-contact health monitoring model based on the internet of things" Eighth international conference on natural computation (ICNC), pp. 506-510, 2012.

[9] S.I. Chaudhry, Y. Wang, J. Concato, T.M. Gill, and H.M. Krumholz, "Patterns of weight change preceding hospitalization for heart failure" Circulation vol. 116, pp. 1549-1554, 2007.

[10] M. Drobics, K.Kreiner and H. Leopold, "Next Generation ICT Platform to Harmonize Medical, Care and Lifestyle Services." ICT Innovations 2015. Springer, Cham, 2016, pp. 275-283, 2016.

[11] J. M. Carroll, Making Use: Scenario-Based Design of Human-Computer Interactions. Cambridge, Massachusetts, MIT press, 2000.

[12] A. Blandford, The Encyclopedia of Human-Computer Interaction. Aarhus, Denmark, Interaction Design Foundation, 2013.

Explicit and Implicit Human Computer Interactions in Ambient Intelligence Environments

From Concepts Towards Concrete Implementations in the Active and Assisted Living Field of Practice

Miroslav Sili
Center for Health & Bioresources
AIT Austrian Institute of Technology GmbH
Giefinggasse 4, 1210 Vienna, Austria
email: Miroslav.Sili@ait.ac.at

Emanuel Sandner & Lukas Roedl
Center for Health & Bioresources
AIT Austrian Institute of Technology GmbH
Giefinggasse 4, 1210 Vienna, Austria
email: Emanuel.Sandner@ait.ac.at, Lukas.Roedl@ait.ac.at

Abstract—**This work presents the design and development process of Ambient Intelligence Environments from the conception phase, over the implementation phase towards the end user perspective. The focus is on different interaction techniques in Ambient Intelligence Environments and their added value for the end user of such a system.**

Keywords-AmI; explicit HCI; eHCI; implicit HCI; iHCI; architecture; Active and Assisted Living; AAL.

I. INTRODUCTION

Ambient Intelligence (AmI) interactions focus on interactions that are supported by, and embedded in, digital equipped environmental settings. As indicated in [1], AmI is a concept that refers to a digital environment that pro-actively, but sensibly, supports people in their daily lives.

In order to reach this goal, it is from utmost importance to consider the contextual information. This is also underlined by Schmidt [2] as follows: "Context and context-awareness are central issues to ambient intelligence. The availability of context and the use of context in interactive applications offer new possibilities to tailor applications and systems on-the-fly to the current situation." The "on-the-fly" adjustment according the current situation is also a central element in adaptive systems [3]. Moreover, AmI systems utilize adaptive systems and the adaptivity factor but with a stronger focus on interactions in digital equipped environmental settings. This, in turn, allows the realization of implicit Human Computer Interactions (iHCI) in ubiquitous and disappearing computing [4]–[6] settings. This is a key element of AmI systems, namely the shift from explicit Human Computer Interaction (eHCI) elements, where users focus on interactions embodied within one single device (e.g., smartphone, tablet device, TV setting, etc.) towards iHCI elements where users can interact with the whole environment. Further on in his work, Schmidt summarizes this juxtaposition of eHCI vs. iHCI as follows:

A. *Explicit Human Computer Interaction (eHCI)*

- The user requests the system to carry out a certain action.
- The action is carried out by the computer, in modern interfaces providing feedback on this process.
- The system responds with an appropriate reply, which in some cases may be empty.

B. *Implict Human Computer Interaction (iHCI)*

- iHCI is the interaction of a human with the environment and with artifacts which is aimed to accomplish a goal. Within this process, the system acquires implicit input from the user and may present implicit output to the user.
- Implicit inputs are actions and behavior of humans, which are done to achieve a goal and are not primarily regarded as interaction with a computer, but captured, recognized and interpret by a computer system as input.
- Implicit output of a computer that is not directly related to an explicit input and which is seamlessly integrated with the environment and the task of the user.

This work focuses on these two interaction types and presents in the first section a literature-based overview about the architectural setting that is needed to realize the eHCI and iHCI approaches within an AmI setting. Section 2 presents a concrete AmI system, which utilizes the mentioned AmI architecture. This development represents the technical point of view regarding AmI systems and the backend, respectively. Section 3 presents two AmI settings from the end user perspective and from the frontend, respectively. This section highlights the eHCI and the iHCI factors where users interact not only with a device but rather with their environment. Section 4 summarizes the work and provides an outlook to future work in this field.

II. BASIC AMI ARCHITECTURE

One remarkable work that summarizes AmI concepts and application was presented by Augusto, et al. [1]. In this work, Augusto presents a general architecture of an AmI system and the corresponding information flow within the system. Figure 1 illustrates components of the general AmI architecture. The top component represents environmental interaction elements. This layer is responsible for the mentioned iHCI aspect but at the same time this layer can also provide eHCI artifacts, for instance, as concrete UIs rendered on a smartphone or on a tablet device. The underlying layer is conducted of Sensors and Actuators. These components are responsible for information transfer from the digital world (in terms of bits and bytes) into the physical world (in terms of physical values, e.g., spatiotemporal sensing and smart-home control), and vice-versa. The next component, the middleware layer, is responsible for the aggregation and the harmonization of sensor data and for the delegation of interventions towards different actuators installed in the environmental setting. This is the core component of an AmI system since it orchestrates the whole information flow. The next component represents the reasoner of the AmI system. In this architecture, Augusto refers to Artificial Intelligence reasoning. Negnevitsky highlights the key characteristic of AI in his work "Artificial intelligence: a guide to intelligent systems" with the following statement: "Artificial intelligence is a science that has defined its goal as making machines do things that would require intelligence if done by human" [7]. At this point, it is doubtful if every AmI Setting and thus if a general AmI architecture really requires this high level of reasoning. Nevertheless, despite of the reasoning level, it is understood, that every AmI system requires a reasoner that retrieves the aggregated and harmonized data form the middleware layer and that delegates interventions towards the middleware layer.

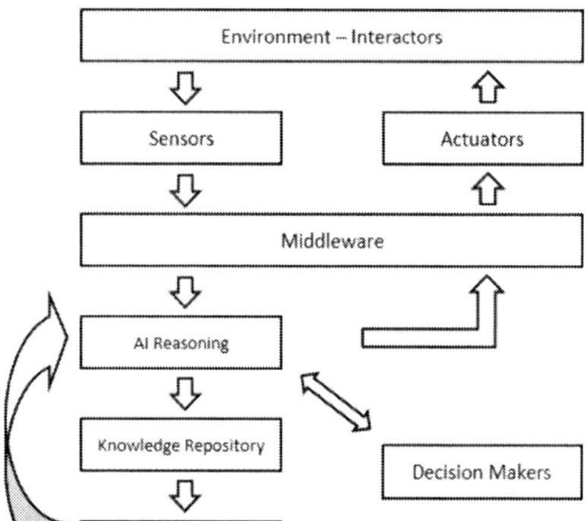

Figure 1. General AmI system architecture and the flow of information [1].

In this work, Augusto uses the phrase "high level decision making process" to explain the remaining components and their interplay. The reasoning is based on the "Decision Makers" component that, for instance, can conclude a set of decision rules, and based on machine learning results produced by the "Discovery and Learning" component. This component requires a "Knowledge Repository" that collects relevant system events and that serves as data provider for the underlying machine learning module.

In the previous section, we have seen that AmI systems relay on physical devices (sensors and actuators) in order to form the Ambient Intelligence environment. Next to the general AmI System architecture, Augusto also presents a generic layout of a Smart Home environment which is equipped with sensors and devices (actuators).

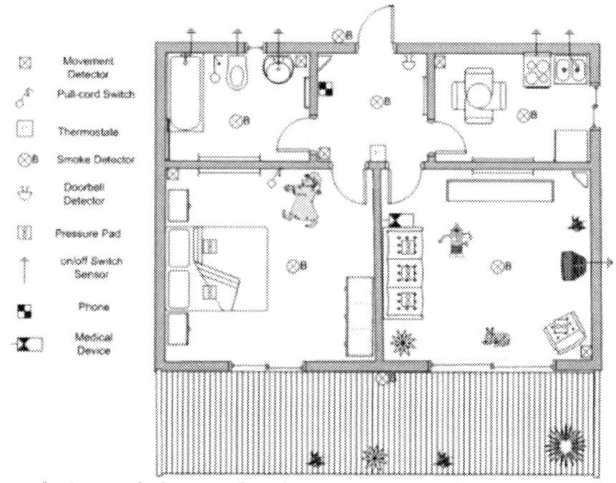

Figure 2. A generic layout of a "Smart Home" enriched with sensors and devices as presented in [1]

Figure 2 illustrates such a Smart Home environment and highlights, that in general, disproportional efforts are needed in order to build an iHCI setting. However, since we are living in a technological driven society it is expected that future technologies and developments will reduce current dominant cost- and complexity factors in building AmI environments. Current products, for instance Apple's HomeKit [8], support this assumption.

III. The HOMER AmI System

Situated in the Active and Assisted Living (AAL) field of practice we have been experiencing the need to build AmI settings in various research projects and developed prototypes [9]–[11]. This resulted in the development of the HOMER [12] AmI system, which can be used across several research projects. The HOMER system utilizes all mentioned components of the general AmI architecture except the AI reasoning on this high sophisticated level. The reasoning in HOMER is bases on a set of finite state machines. Thus, HOMER provides in the first step rule-based reasoning, but it also provides interfaces for external components that build the knowledge repository and the machine learning components. However, Figure 3 illustrates the rule-based reasoning which utilizes finite state machines. States can trigger various interventions and the transitions have a large set of configurable conditions which need to be fulfilled in order to change the system state from one state into another. This example illustrates only one finite state machine within the system. It needs to be mentioned that the HOMER AmI setting supports a large set of finite state machines which are concurrently considered in the decision-making process.

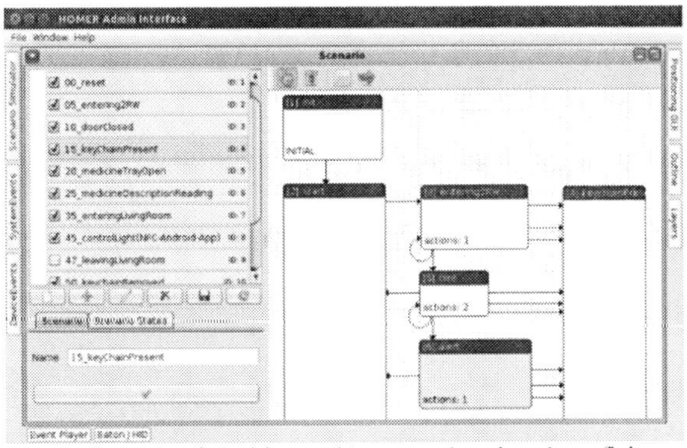

Figure 3. Example of decision making procedure based on finite state machines [12].

Despite the reasoning and the decision-making process, HOMER incorporates various sensors and devices responsible for the communication with the physical environment. Table I illustrates an excerpt of used devices and their purpose within the HOMER AmI environment.

TABLE I. COMMUNICATION WITH PHYSICAL DEVICES IN THE HOMER AMI ENVIRONMENT

Purpose	***Technology/Protocols***
Motion detection	PIR Sensors (KNX, enOcean, Homematic, xComfort)
Indoor localization	RSSI-based localization (iBeacon), PIR based
Smart Home control	Actuators (KNX, enOcean, Homematic, RfxTrx, Tradfri)
Ambient lighting	Smart Lights (Philips Hue, Tradfri)
Energy consumption	Energy consumption sensors (Homematic, xComfort)
Water valve control	Sprinkler actuators (OpenSprinkler)
Environmental Sensing	Air quality, Temperature, Humidity, Barometric, Rain or Wind sensors (RfxTrx, Oregon Scientific)
Activity Sensing	Binary sensors, smart floor, window sensors
Medical Device communication	Weighing scale, blood pressure measurement devices (Near Field Communication - NFC, Bluetooth)
Event tracking	Device usage- based event tracking
Object identification	sensing & control, e.g., door opener, key reminder (NFC)
TV as Interaction device	IR, HDMI-CEC & SmartTV-based

The table is not meant to be holistic, but rather to highlight that the development of AmI environments can be a quite complex procedure. In HOMER, a separate hardware abstraction layer enables the various modules to interact with each other and the rest of the system. HOMER itself utilizes the ISO/IEEE 11073-10471 standard for communication.

IV. THE END USER PERSPECTIVE

Previous sections focused on the AmI concept, AmI architecture and the concrete manifestation based on the presented HOMER AmI system. This section focusses on the end user perspective and highlights eHCI and iHCI aspects within AmI settings.

As already highlighted in the previous section, AmI systems require Smart Home settings. In Figure 2 a generic layout of a "Smart Home" was presented. This illustration is similar to the HOMER setting, since HOMER also supports a representation of the current status within the Smart Home environment. Figure 4 illustrates this representation on a wall-mounted display. The figure highlights the floor plan of a demonstration setting conducted of two living rooms (lower part) and the hall way (upper part). The depicted dots within the floor plan illustrate installed sensors and actuators. Any activity originated form these devices are instantly updated in the GUI. Next to the visual representation, HOMER supports also speech synthesis as an interaction medium in order to inform the user regarding critical situations using the acoustical interaction modality. This is highlighted by the speaker which is located on the top of the wall-mounted display.

Figure 4. Smart Home status representation on a wall-mounted display including a speaker for the HOMER system speech synthesis.

In addition to the wall-mounted representation, the HOMER GUI can be rendered on any mobile device within this setting but also on TV-devices. This represents the classical eHCI approach where the user requests the system to carry out a certain action and where the system responds with an appropriate reply. As pointed out earlier, AmI environments additionally support the iHCI approach, where users interact with the environment rather than with devices. In the HOMER setting, an iHCI is, for instance, the door or the window opening action. This action is recognized by the system and might cause an intervention by the system if a critical condition is met. Such a critical condition is, for instance, the state where the user has forgotten to close/lock the door after entering the apartment. The system provides in such a case an intervention via the mentioned speech synthesis feature or via a push notification which will be displayed on user's smartphone.

As mentioned before, in our AAL field of practice, we have been utilizing HOMER in various projects and developments. The following example illustrates eHCI and iHCI aspects of AmI environments based on the research project RelaxedCare [9],[13],[14].

The project was performed between May 2013 and April 2016 and was targeting the development of an interactive system for informal caregiver and their assisted persons. The goal of the project was to provide a solution which can reduce the necessity of regularly checking the status of a person in need of care, living at home. Although the project has finished years ago, its concept still represents the state-of-the-art approach regarding AmI, eHCI and iHCI. Figure 5 illustrates the basic idea of the RelaxedCare system. It depicts the AmI setting installed at the assisted person and the communication channels towards the informal caregiver. The overall goal of the project was to provide iHCI artifacts that derive a wellbeing state of the person in need of care. The assisted person primarily interacts with their living environment and less with explicit devices. On the other hand, the informal caregiver utilizes technologies such as the smartphone or an ambient light device to perceive the overall wellbeing state of their assisted person and to start the dialog with the remote person. This setting represents a mixed setting that utilizes eHCI artifacts (smartphone, RelaxedCare cube) and iHCI artifacts (the interactive picture frame, the ambient light device and the RelaxedCare cube).

Figure 5. The RelaxedCare idea depicting the AmI environment in the top half of the image and the communication channels at the bottom half of the image.

This iHCI vs. eHCI juxtaposition becomes even clearer if we take the final prototype into account that is depicted in Figure 6. The figure illustrates the mentioned ambient light device that can be installed on both sides, on the informal caregiver side and on the assisted person's side. The ambient lighting represents the overall wellbeing state of the assisted person. This wellbeing state is derived from activity level, social interaction and daily life routine data, which in turn are provided by the AmI setting.

Figure 6. The RelaxedCare cube prototype that provides the overall wellbeing state of the assisted person via ambient lighting.

Thus, iHCI artifacts are used twofold: (1) to convey the wellbeing information and (2) to collect data for deriving the wellbeing state. Additionally, the solution provides eHCI artifacts by utilizing NFC-based tangible buttons which, when placed on the top of the RelaxedCare cube, cause a concrete communication action towards the remote user or a user-triggered change of the well-being status. Finally, the solution provides several predefined actions such as "please call me", "I feel good/bad" or the emotion in term of "I'm thinking of you". This information is transferred to the remote person to their smartphone and to their ambient lightning device. Here, and once again, the remote user utilizes both iHCI and eHCI factors for the information gathering and for the communication establishment.

V. Conclusion and Further Work

This work presented the design process from the conceptualization of AmI systems based on a general architecture, over to the manifestation of an AmI system based on the HOMER platform, towards the utilization of an AmI system demonstrated by the RelaxedCare project. Moreover, this work highlighted one of the key aspects of AmI systems, which is, next to the context awareness, also the provision of explicit HCI artifacts and implicit HCI artifacts. In addition to these positive aspects, the work also underlined that the design and the development of AmI systems can be a time-consuming, costly and complex process. Nevertheless, current technological developments, as highlighted earlier in Section 2, indicate that these negative factors can be alleviated in the near feature.

Thus, with respect to future work, our focus will be the incorporation of such off-the-shelf technologies and the stronger focus on the decision-making process including its subparts, namely the enhancement of the knowledge base representation and the enhancement of machine learning algorithms.

References

[1] J. C. Augusto and P. McCullagh, "Ambient intelligence: Concepts and applications," Computer Science and Information Systems, vol. 4, pp. 1–27, 2007.

[2] A. Schmidt, "Interactive context-aware systems interacting with ambient intelligence," Ambient intelligence, vol. 159, pp. 159–178, 2005.

[3] C. Mayer et al., "A comparative study of systems for the design of flexible user interfaces," Journal of Ambient Intelligence and Smart Environments, vol. 8, pp. 125–148, 2016.

[4] N. Streitz and P. Nixon, "The disappearing computer," Communications-ACM, vol. 48, pp. 32–35, 2005.

[5] M. Weiser, "The computer for the 21st century.," Mobile Computing and Communications Review, vol. 3, pp. 3–11, 1999.

[6] M. Weiser and J. S. Brown, "The coming age of calm technology," Beyond calculation, Springer, pp. 75–85, 1997.

[7] M. Negnevitsky, "Artificial intelligence: a guide to intelligent systems" , Pearson Education, 2005.

[8] A. Inc., *iOS - Home Accessories - Apple (UK)*. [Online]. Available from: https://www.apple.com/uk/ios/home/accessories 2018.10.24

[9] M. Morandell, S. Dittenberger, A. Koscher, E. Sandner, and M. Sili, "The simpler the better: How the user-inspired innovation process (UIIP) improved the development of RelaxedCare–the entirely new way of communicating and caring," International Conference of Design, User Experience, and Usability, Springer, pp. 382–391, 2016.

[10] C. Siegel, B. Prazak-Aram, J. Kropf, M. Kundi, and T. Dorner, "Evaluation of a modular scalable system for silver-ager located in assisted living homes in Austria–study protocol of the ModuLAAr ambient assisted living project," BMC public health, vol. 14, p. 736, 2014.

[11] F. Palumbo, D. La Rosa, and E. Ferro, "Stigmergy-based Long-Term Monitoring of Indoor Users Mobility in Ambient Assisted Living Environments: the DOREMI Project Approach.," AI* AAL@ AI* IA, pp. 18–32, 2016.

[12] T. Fuxreiter et al., "A modular platform for event recognition in smart homes," e-Health Networking Applications and Services (Healthcom), 12th IEEE International Conference on, IEEE, pp. 1–6, 2010.

[13] M. Morandell, "Relaxedcare: How Informal Caregivers Stay Informed and Connected in a Really Easy Way," Alzheimer's & Dementia: The Journal of the Alzheimer's Association, vol. 12, p. P157, 2016.

[14] T.R.P. Consortium, *RelaxedCare | connecting people in care situations*. [Online]. Available from: http://www.relaxedcare.eu/de 2018.10.24

Improving Interdisciplinary Communication – Use Case Focused User Interaction Diagram 2.0

Daniela E. Ströckl, Daniela Krainer, Elena Oberrauner
Active & Assisted Living – Research Unit of Carinthia University of Applied Sciences
Klagenfurt, Austria
e-mail: {d.stroeckl, d.krainer, e.oberrauner}@fh-kaernten.at

Abstract— **In this paper, we present the results of further research according to a communication improvement method within projects with interdisciplinary disposition. This method was used in the Active and Assisted Living (AAL) pilot-region project Smart VitAALity, to encourage elderly people to interact with state of the art technologies and formulate their needs. In addition to various research partners (computer science, economics and health management), business partners and Non-Profit Organizations (NPOs), end-users are also involved, and all these project partners speak a different language, according to their profession. The Use Case focused User Interaction Diagram 2.0 should provide a non-technical translation for every stakeholder independent of their prior knowledge to enhance the development process and capture various aspects, ideas, and suggestions for improvements and, furthermore, it should represent the interaction needs of elderly people. Therefore, the diagram was evaluated by elderly people to improve the feedback method.**

Keywords - Interaction Design; Human-system Interface; Interaction Diagram; Communication method; AAL.

I. INTRODUCTION

During applied research projects, it is common that communication takes place between different stakeholders with diverse background knowledge. These stakeholders often use the same terms with different meanings; to avoid misunderstandings, the Use Case Focused User Interaction Diagram [1] (UC-UI-Diagram 1.0) was developed according to the development process of systems with a human-system interface. This tool improves the communication base in interdisciplinary projects and gives every stakeholder a quick overview of the ongoing interface development per use case.

Referring to the first version of the chart notation, the Use Case Focused User Interaction Diagram 2.0 (UC-UI-Diagram 2.0) was developed with the approach to minimize the notation elements in order to improve the learning curve for understanding the diagrams. Therefore, the number of notation elements was decimated from eight to three and the elements were adjusted according to the UML 2.5 [2] standard element design. One of the reasons for the element design change was that the used element design of the UC-UI-Diagram 1.0 required different color expressions and the contrast and discriminability was not useable for a possible involvement of older adults with visual impairments. To also use the UC-UI-Diagram for this stakeholder group during the development process, the idea of the pre-evaluated element design of the UML 2.5 interaction diagrams (sequence diagram and communication diagram [2]) was used. This makes it possible to create the diagrams with common diagram drawing tools like Microsoft Visio, because the element designs are pre-installed and, furthermore, computer scientists are familiar with them and can also use the diagrams during the implementation into the system.

In the project Smart VitAALity, an Active and Assisted Living (AAL) pilot region project in Austria (Carinthia), the UC-UI-Diagram 2.0 method was initially used to improve the communication between technical and non-technical stakeholders. The involved stakeholder group is an interdisciplinary consortium of researchers in health management, economics, computer science and engineering, as well as Small and Medium-sized Enterprises (SMEs) with the emphasis of technical development and NPOs as caregivers. The entire project team was involved in the development process of the use cases. To extend the perspective of each use case, the UC-UI-Diagram 2.0 is additionally used. This information is provided on a shared platform to every stakeholder and, based on this, everyone can make proposals for improvements. To let the user group participate in the development process, it is necessary to evaluate the used tool with their prior-knowledge and usability. Therefore, during the Smart VitAALity project, the UC-UI Diagram 2.0 was evaluated and the results are presented in this paper.

The rest of the paper is structured as follows. In Section II, we discuss the materials and method. Section III presents our results. Section IV addresses improvement and discussion. We conclude this paper in Section V.

II. MATERIALS AND METHODS

This section explains the background for the UC-UI Diagram 2.0. Furthermore, it presents the evaluation strategy according to the human-centered design approach [3].

A. UML 2.5 Communication and Sequence Diagram

The concept of time-related interaction between entities, as well as the illustration of relations between entities, can be realized with communication diagrams in combination with sequence terms. Because of its structure, this diagram extension is hard to understand for non-technical stakeholders. To get a quick overview of the different interactions, the UML standard uses a nesting strategy.

$$1.2b.1: function2(param1, param2) \quad (1)$$

As shown in (1), the notation for communication diagram interactions with sequence terms is realized. The designation 1.2b.1 means: the first interaction in the content led to a second interaction which was a parallel interaction denoted with b (the other parallel interactions will get an "a" or a "c"). The interaction after the parallel one (2b) will be the executed interaction in this example with function2, which contains two parameters. This can be hard to understand if the usage of such UML standards is not a daily business. To ease the understanding of the interaction diagram, two measures were undertaken:

1. Simplify interaction sequences: no parallel interactions illustrated with characters or complicated numbering to show dependencies between interactions
2. Context change: the interaction diagram is specific for one named use case – to make it easier to understand

The UC-UI Diagram 2.0 should use the idea of use case based interaction of the prior 1.0 version of the diagram and combine it with the idea of the time and relation related interaction concept of UML 2.5. Furthermore, the diagram should be developed in a way that even non-technical experts should be able to understand and give feedback to improve the navigation strategy.

B. UC-UI Diagram 2.0 Evaluation Strategy

For the evaluation of the developed UC-UI Diagram 2.0, an assessment was made with the aim to analyze the diagrams to determine acceptability, understanding and potential areas for improvement. The evaluation process can be divided into the following five phases.

The participants of the chosen user group were selected based on their age - between 50 and 75 years. In the first phase (**step 1**) of the evaluation, the participants completed the TA-EG survey [4] ("Technology Affinity for Electronic Devices") which is a tool to assess the technical affinity and serves to determine the attitude towards electronic devices of the participants. The TE-AG consists of 19 items structured in four subscales "Enthusiasm", "Competency", "Positive impacts", "Negative impacts" when dealing with electronic devices like mobile phone, computer, TV, etc.

The second phase (**step 2**) was about the comprehension of the diagram. For this purpose, the developed diagram with a corresponding legend, was shown to the test persons for the first time. Since it is a UC-UI Diagram, the use case "show weather forecast" was chosen, because the participants may be familiar with this scenario from daily routines. The task of this phase was to understand the diagram with the enclosed legend after the documents were explained in detail.

The next step (**step 3**) in the evaluation process was about the graphical representation of the interaction elements in the diagram, such as buttons or text elements. Therefore, the participants were asked to design a mock-up based on the current use case. The emphasis in this assignment was to see if the participants get a picture in their minds according to the diagram elements and if they distinguish different element types (e.g., text, buttons, etc.). After the completion of this task, the created mock-up design was compared to an existing design representing the same use case, and the results were discussed.

In the fourth phase (**step 4**), an incomplete interaction diagram was presented, representing the use case "emergency call". In this scenario, one element was omitted deliberately: A "Cancel" button that prevents the user to cancel a particular part of the scenario. The goal was to look more closely at the navigation paths within the diagram to find the mistake.

Finally, in the fifth phase (**step 5**), the test persons were asked if they had already worked with a UC-UI Diagram and if such a diagram could be a straightforward way to display navigation paths. Furthermore, the participants were asked about the difficulties while working with the diagrams during the evaluation process. In the end, suggestions for potential improvements were discussed.

The used language for all documents was German. The session had one hour duration.

III. RESULTS

Within this section, the results of the diagram conceptualization and the evaluation are presented.

A. UC-UI Diagram 2.0

To get a step further into the understanding improvement, the diagram notation was reversed from the 1.0 version and, according to the feedback of project partners, the learning curve of the elements was too high. Hence, the main ideas of the sequential and communication diagram [2] are combined in the 2.0 version.

Diagram Notation

Based on the feedback regarding the chart notation of the UC-UI Diagram 1.0, the used elements needed to be reduced. From eight elements, the reduction leads to three elements – because it is not necessary for non-technical stakeholders to distinguish between elements like external influencer, decisions or merges by diagram design. For any additional information, the elements will get a unique understandable label.

As shown in Figure 1, there are three elements to distinguish. The use case container includes all possible interactions of a specific use case. The agent container represents agents like views, people, interaction elements like buttons or checkboxes as well as descriptions. The user can interact in different ways with the agents; the agent container represents a human being itself. Every agent has a specific non-technical labeling. The agents can be nested into each other.

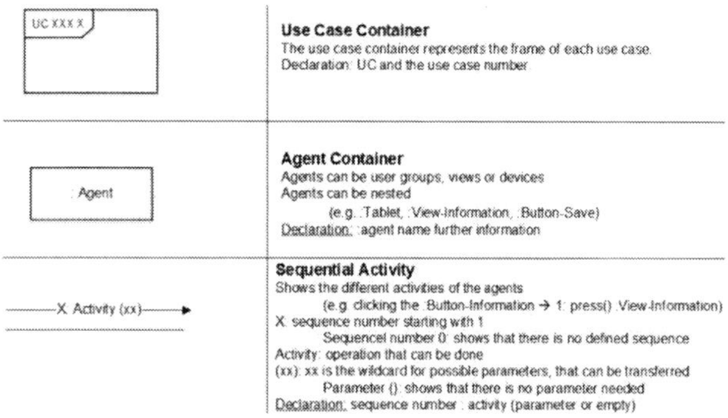

Figure 1. UC-UI Diagram 2.0 diagram notation (English translation). Description of the three used elements: use case container, agent container, and sequential activity.

In the case of a software project like Smart VitAALity, a tablet application is implemented. Every application shows different views to a user and every view contains different elements, like text or buttons. In this example, the first agent will be the view, and in the view agent container, the agent container for the button is nested.

This interaction diagram type focuses on human-system interaction and, therefore, the sequential activities are optimized. Users are able to do one interaction after another – real parallelization is no human possible interaction so no special notation is needed [5]. This type of diagram (UC-UI diagram 2.0) focuses on human-system interactions; all interactions a user can do with the system and the main function is displayed. In the following, one sample scenario is given:

Scenario: the user enters some content into a text-field. Instead of representing every key down interaction, only the save-interaction is shown. Moreover, further distinctions and system-to-system interactions in the front- and backend like "content send to backend" → "backend receives content" → "content stored in the database" have been excluded from the diagram.

Therefore, sequential activities are numbered one after another with simple counting one, two, and three. After the counting, the interaction receives a function name and a possible parameter. This parameter can be a decision parameter as for a checkbox (option 1 and 2) or in some cases, it can be empty.

In comparison to the UC-UI Diagram 1.0, the second version renounces to any color usage as well as different line style. Furthermore, the diagram has the highest possible contrast according to the black/white diagram notation; according to the conformance stage of the Web Content Accessibility Guidelines – WCAG 2.1 [6] this is needed for a barrier-free usage. This makes it easier for people with vision impairments (color blindness or ametropia) to understand the diagrams – and according to AAL projects, it is one aspect for the inclusion of elderly people to minimize the barriers and to enhance the participation during the implementation phase.

In the Smart VitAALity project, 71 use cases are defined. All use cases are written with the use case template of Alistair Cockburn [7]. For every single use case, the different possible procedures (standard procedure and multiple alternative procedures) are explained. This helps on the one hand the developers to have an exact implementation guideline and furthermore it increases the reading flow and understanding for non-technicians.

The strategy used in the project was to combine the use case template of Cockburn with a method that gives a quick overview of all possible interactions. Therefore, the UC-UI Diagram 2.0 was used.

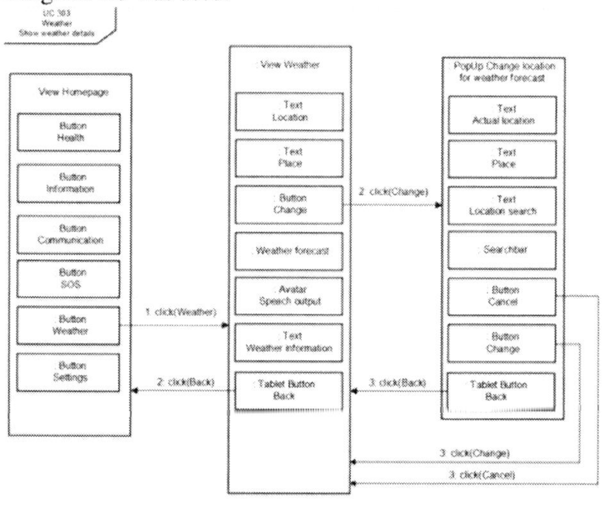

Figure 2. Example of the use case "UC 303 Show weather details" of the Smart VitAALity project. Shown are the different views of a tablet application to realize a weather forecast.

As shown in Figure 2, the first agent container on the left ":View-Homepage" includes the possibility to do more interactions like clicking on Button-Information or Button-SOS, but the UC-UI Diagram 2.0 is in context of a pre-defined use case "UC 303 Weather – Show weather details". This helps to minimize and regulate the shown interactions and to get a clean and neatly arranged interaction overview. Nonetheless, it should represent the whole context of each view to give the user the big picture and an idea whether the navigation in the context would be understandable.

B. *Evaluation Results*

For evaluation purposes, five people (3 female, 2 male) were tested according to the five-step evaluation strategy chosen. The youngest participant was 51 years old and the oldest 73 years. All these people are living in the urban-rural area of Klagenfurt and Villach in Carinthia – Austria. According to their pre-knowledge of using technical devices like smartphones, computers or tablet computers, 4/5 people have a smartphone and tablet computer and 5/5 people have contact with at least one technical device.

Step 1: TA-EG

At the beginning of the evaluation process, the participants were asked to complete the TA-EG questionnaire with a five-level Likert response format (strongly disagree – strongly agree). For each participant, the mean values of all items of the individual subscales "Enthusiasm" for electronic devices (5 items), perceived "Competency" (4 items), perceived "Positive impacts" (5 items) and perceived "Negative impacts" (5 items), were calculated to get an overview of the technology affinity. Table I shows the mean value and the standard deviation of the technology affinity for electronic devices of all five participants, where value 5 is the maximum and means "strong agreement" and value 1 "strong disagreement".

TABLE I: RESULTS OF TECHNOLOGY AFFINITY QUESTIONNAIRE FOR ELECTRONIC DEVICES (N=5); MEAN VALUE 1…STRONGLY DISAGREE – 5…STRONGLY AGREE

Subscale of TA-EG	Mean Value	Standard Deviation
Enthusiasm for electronic devices	3.4	0.9
Perceived Competency	3.2	0.7
Perceived negative impacts	2.3	0.5
Perceived positive impacts	4.4	0.3

On average, the participants have a "neutral" response ("neither-nor" agreement) on "Enthusiasm" for electronic devices, with a high variance and range from slightly disagree to strongly agree on "Enthusiasm". The results for the perceived "Competency" are similar and show on average a "neither-nor" agreement on "Competency", with a range from slightly disagree to slightly agree.

For the subscales perceived "Negative impacts" and "Positive impacts", on average the participants show a slight disagreement on perceived "Negative impacts" when using electronic devices and a moderate / strong agreement on perceived "Positive impacts" when using electronic devices.

Overall, and besides varying agreement to "Enthusiasm" and "Competency", the attitude towards usage of electronic devices is positive.

Step 2: Use Case "Weather Forecast" + Diagram Key

After some general instructions, the UC-UI Diagram 2.0 example was shown to the participants and discussed according to the use case on the one hand and the different elements on the other. Furthermore, the diagram key was given to the participants to have a look at it. The following results, presented in Table II, are evaluated:

TABLE II. QUESTIONS, RESULTS, AND REMARKS ACCORDING TO THE WEATHER FORECAST USE CASE.

Question	Result & Remarks
Is the diagram key helpful to understand the UC-UI Diagram 2.0?	4/5 said it was not necessary or would confuse them 1/5 understood it, but an example and a short spoken introduction were preferred.
Is the "Weather forecast" -UI Diagram understandable?	5/5 mentioned that it was clear for them
Do you know what a View is?	3/5 answered right 2/5 people told after further questioning that they did not recognize that every view was a different page.

Step 3: Mock-Ups Use Case "Weather Forecast"

The next step was to draw the different views shown in the UC-UI Diagram on sheets of paper. 4/5 participants did not really want to draw anything at first because they thought they were not talented enough in the drawing. Two out of this group disliked the exercise a lot, they just drew anything but talked more about the results. After their drawing exercise, the real mock-ups for the UC-UI Diagram were shown and the differences between their interpretation and the real mock-up discussed. The results of this step are shown in Table III.

TABLE III. EXERCISE ISSUES, RESULTS, AND REMARKS ACCORDING TO THE MOCK UP DRAWING OF THE WEATHER FORECAST USE CASE

Exercise issues	Results & Remarks
Allocation of elements	4/5 started drawing on the upper left corner and drew very few elements. After telling them that they had enough space and more than one paper, they started drawing bigger elements.

Symbols or text elements	4/5 drew predominantly symbols instead of text for the buttons; 1/5 was the total opposite. After re-asking them why, they started mixing more because they had the feeling that it was not right what they are doing.
Label & drawing	5/5 drew all elements in boxes like they were drawn in the UC-UI Diagram. Asking why: they didn't care while they were drawing if it was a text or button and they could not do it better.
Labeling	5/5 could not differentiate between texts. It was not clear if the text was a label or a text-input or some information. All participants had problems in drawing the ": View Weather" because of this issue.
Wording	5/5 did not know what an "Avatar" was and 4/5 did not know at first what a "PopUp" was. After explaining it, it became clear but they could not work with these words.
Showing the mock-up	5/5 connected the mock-up to the diagram; 3/5 told that it looked nice and that they had something similar in mind but they were not able to draw like that.

Step 4: Use Case "Emergency Call"

The second use case shown was "Emergency call", and it was prepared with a mistake – a navigation trap; the participants needed to identify that they were caught in a loop in one view and could not navigate to another view anymore. Furthermore, they should explain what they saw in a Think Aloud manor. The following results in Table IV were detected:

TABLE IV. EXERCISE ISSUES, RESULTS, AND REMARKS ACCORDING TO THE EMERGENCY CALL USE CASE

Exercise issues	Results & Remarks
Explaining the use case	5/5 could explain what they saw on the diagram
Evaluate the navigation process	3/5 started to evaluate the given navigation strategy and they focused on how to improve the "Emergency call" as such.
Mistake detection	3/5 could find the mistake by themselves; two needed some hints to get it 3/5 told that they first thought it was no mistake because on tablet computers they always had the "Home"-button option to cancel, (not shown in the diagram).
Drawing mistake improvement	4/5 mentioned the mistake with speech, 1/5 participant drew a button as it should be.

Step 5: Reflection

After all the tasks were done, the last part of the evaluation was to get some reflection based on pre-defined questions. These questions, together with results and remarks, are shown in Table V.

TABLE V. QUESTIONS, RESULTS, AND REMARKS ACCORDING TO THE REFLECTION OF THE UC-UI DIAGRAM 2.0 EVALUATION

Questions	Results & Remarks
Are you used to such diagram representations?	4/5 never used such diagrams or other similar ones before. 1 participant had experience in process management (former occupation).
Is it a good method to represent navigation purposes and could it improve/replace written manuals?	4/5 thought it was a clearly structured way to describe navigation processes; 2/5 would have preferred this description according to written manuals 3/5 would have suggested it as a supplement to written manuals
Could there be difficulties by using the UC-UI Diagram 2.0?	5/5 wanted a clear wording according to interaction and non-interaction elements like the text element. The word text alone was not clear enough. 1/5 said that maybe non-technical affine people could have problems in general with technical diagrams.
Have you had any difficulties using the diagram?	5/5 mentioned the wording of the element; it was not clear enough 1/5 said that the elements were too close to each other
Do you think you are able to give feedback according to the navigation strategy (mistakes or improvement)?	5/5 said that they thought, after an explanation of the diagram, that they were able to give feedback or improve the use case navigation strategy. 3/5 already did it in the second use case;
Do you have now ideas for improvement?	2/5 mentioned that there was no need for the relations to be labeled with "click" 1/5 mentioned that all Anglicisms should be avoided 2/5 mentioned that non-interaction elements should be removed 1/5 mentioned - fewer rectangles would be better, elements could be combined

The results shown in Table V influence further research and improvement of the diagram.

IV. IMPROVEMENT & DISCUSSION

The intention to include the end-users from the very first steps during a development process should reduce misguided implementation. Therefore, new soft- and/or hardware tools enable users to participate in an appropriate way. That means that non-experts need to get a big picture of the development processes even before design issues are developed. To get feedback about the navigation and/or interaction concept, it is necessary to work with a tool that end-users easily understand so that they can concentrate on the main topic – to evaluate interaction proposals.

To develop such a tool and to prove that it is working for a certain user group, an evaluation was undertaken. Referring to the results of that evaluation, three major issues could be identified, which should be improved in future before working with the diagrams intensively.

Language

The element labeling still has the proper wording for the user group. The improvement should clarify if an element is an interaction element or not. Regarding the participants, maybe all non-interaction elements should be removed. If such elements are in the diagram, they should be labelled clearly, so that there are no misunderstandings possible. Easy language should be (German: Leichte Sprache [8]) used and all the English terms should be avoided. This could increase the acceptability and usability of the participants.

Diagram key

The diagram key may be important for research purposes, but for users it is not relevant at all. They are confused because of the given explanations. It is easier for the user group to give a simple example, maybe with a mock-up, and/or explain it before they use it in feedback sessions.

Relation-labelling

The participants did not notice the labeling referring to the click-action and two of them mentioned that it was not relevant and could be removed. This should be evaluated again; maybe if there was more than just click interaction it could also be relevant for the user group.

As for now, the UC-UI Diagram 2.0 version is used in AAL projects like Smart VitAALity. In the current development stage, it is possible to give elderly user groups who are non-technical a tool that helps them give feedback to the prior-defined navigation strategy. Still, there is room for improvement according to the prior mentioned topics with language leading the way. The next step for improving the diagram will be a survey (maybe online) according to the wording topic; the study will be supported by a linguist.

V. CONCLUSION

This paper shows the evaluation results of a simple diagram language (UC-UI Diagram 2.0), that should assist the participation of elderly users during development processes in AAL projects. According the results, this type of diagram will also be used in other projects and it will be improved iteratively, maybe with a bigger group of participants, to make it even more applicable.

ACKNOWLEDGMENT

We want to thank all those who have contributed to our UC-UI diagram 2.0 evaluation within the project Smart VitAALity. The pilot region Smart VitAALity (grant no. 858380) is co-financed by funds of the benefit programme from the Austrian Federal Ministry for Transport, Innovation and Technology (bmvit).

REFERENCES

[1] D. Krainer, D. E. Ströckl, and J. Oberzaucher, "Use Case Focused User-Interaction Diagram – A Communication Tool within AAL Projects" in: PETRA '17: Proceedings of the 10th International Conference on Pervasive Technologies Related to Assistive Environments, 21-23 Jun 2017, Island of Rhodes, Greece, S. 193.196, 2017

[2] Object Management Group (OMG); OMG Unified Modeling Language – Version 2.5; http://www.omg.org/spec/UML/2.5, 2015 [retrieved: September, 2018]

[3] Germany.ISO. 9241-210: 2010. "Ergonomics of human system interaction-Part 210: Human-centred design for interactive systems." International Standardization Organization (ISO). Switzerland, 2010

[4] K. Karrer, C. Glaser, C. Clemens, and C. Bruder, „Capture technology attraction– the survey TA-EG". Original Title: "Technologieaffinität erfassen – der Fragebogen TA-EG" In A. Lichtenstein, C. Stößel und C. Clemens (Hrsg.), Der Mensch im Mittelpunkt technischer Systeme. 8. Werkstatt Mensch-Maschine Systeme (ZMMS Spektrum, Reihe 22, Nr. 29, S. 196-201). Düsseldorf: VDI Verlag GmbH, 2009

[5] T. Schubert, "The central attentional limitation and executive control." Front. Biosci. 13, 3569-3580. 10.2741/2950, 2008

[6] World Wide Wep Consortium (W3C). "Web Contenct Accessibility Guidelines (WCAG) 2.1"; https://www.w3c.org/TR/WCAG21/, 2017 [retrieved: September, 2018]

[7] A. Cockburn, „Effectively creating Use Cases." Original Title: "Use Cases effektiv erstellen." MITP Verlach, 2003 ISBN 3-8266-1344-9, 2003

[8] U. Bredel and C. Maaß, „Simple Language: theoretical essentials. Orientation for the practice" Original: „Leichte Sprache: Theoretische Grundlagen. Orientierung für die Praxis." Duden. ISBN: 978-3-411-75616-2, 2016

Review of User Interfaces for Caregivers in Ambient Assisted Living

Alena Brennan*, Keara Barrett*, Caroline Byrne*, Gregory M. P. O'Hare† and Ailish Kavanagh*
*Department of Computing
Institute of Technology Carlow, Co.Carlow, Ireland
Email: {c00187707, keara.barrett, caroline.byrne, c00206130}@itcarlow.ie
†School of Computer Science
University College Dublin (UCD) Belfield,
Dublin 4, Ireland
Email: gregory.ohare@ucd.ie

Abstract—**As the world's population ages, Ambient Assisted Living becomes a topic of considerable interest. At present, multimodal user interfaces in Ambient Assisted Living systems are an important research area. The contribution of this paper is to ascertain the needs of caregivers and family members, pertaining to the activities of daily living information of the elderly, discuss how these needs are best presented, and analyse existing user interfaces in Ambient Assisted Living systems based on the identified criteria. This paper concludes by highlighting the scarcity of research in the area of user interfaces and outlining future work to enrich the design of user interfaces.**

Keywords–Ambient Assisted Living; User Interfaces for Caregivers; Activities of Daily Living.

I. INTRODUCTION

The world's population continues to age rapidly as people live longer. It is predicted that by 2050 the number of people aged 65 years and over will exceed the younger population for the first time in history [1]. In this context, Ambient Assisted Living (AAL) extends the time period during which the elderly can live independently in their homes using Information Technology and reduces the overall burden on family caregivers.

Numerous AAL projects facilitate independent living for the elderly. The User Interface (UI) is an integral part of these projects, as UIs facilitate interaction between the user and the AAL system. The majority of users' interaction with computing systems occurs through a graphical UI [2]. UI design that addresses the needs of caregivers is critical to technology acceptance, adoption and consumer satisfaction [3].

UI design requirements are dependent on the type of users for which the interface is intended. In AAL, several types of users, or stakeholders, are distinguished [4]:

- The elderly: people who need assistance to live independently. They are considered to have the greatest stake in the success of the AAL vision;
- The family members and the elderly person's loved ones: they act as informal caregivers. The responsibility for caring for the elderly often falls upon them;
- Formal medical caregivers: people who are paid to give care. AAL helps the caregivers to use their limited resources in a more effective manner.

The needs of the first group of stakeholders, the elderly, have been studied thoroughly. For example, Johnson and Finn [5] present an extensive study of age-related changes in vision, motor control, hearing, speech, cognition, and they offer UI design guidelines. Dodd et al. [2] identify the physical, cognitive, and computer-related issues the elderly experience with UIs created to assist them and review the existing solutions.

However, UI research is limited for caregivers/family members, even though caregiving is regarded as a complex or even stressful activity and can cause adverse physical and mental health consequences [6]. Therefore, these technologies for helping caregivers/family members require more attention, as they offer a technological aid which may enable them to concentrate on their unique health needs and achieve a healthier lifestyle.

This paper will concentrate on caregivers/family members and their needs in AAL UI design. The contribution of this paper is to review, evaluate, and critique UIs for caregivers/family members in AAL systems that present summarised Activities of Daily Living (ADLs) information in an effective way. This paper is organised as follows. Section II defines the kind of information caregivers/family members need for reassurance that their elderly loved ones are undertaking their daily routines. Section II further describes how these needs are best presented in UIs for caregivers in AAL. Section III presents the UIs in AAL systems that provide assistance to caregivers/family members of elderly people, and analyses them based on the criteria described in Section II. The conclusions and future work are outlined in Section IV.

II. ADL INFORMATION AND PRESENTATION METHODS FOR CAREGIVERS OF THE ELDERLY

The first subsection will discuss the needs of caregivers/family members pertaining to the ADL information that UIs in AAL present. The visual methods which can be employed to present ADL information will be discussed in the following subsection.

A. ADL Information for Caregivers/Family Members

ADLs are routine actions that are performed by individuals every day and are essential for independent life. Correct ADL measurement is significant for the management of healthcare in aging societies.

1) Sleep: Sleep is vital for overall health at any age. The elderly who do not acquire good-quality sleep can suffer from a range of sleep disorders, for example, insomnia and sleep apnoea. Family members wish to be aware of their loved ones' quality and quantity of sleep as poor sleeping patterns have health implications. If an elderly person experiences multiple consecutive nights of poor sleep, their family members want to be informed, so that they can intervene if necessary [7]. Poor quality sleep reduces mobility, communication, and social contact with other people. The duration of day sleep, the length of uninterrupted sleep at night, the number of times, and for how long the elderly person gets up in the night are characteristics of the quantity of sleep [8]. To collect sleep data the following information needs to be logged: time of day when alarm is set, scheduled wake up time, time of day when the elderly person goes to bed, sleep duration, sleep efficiency, amount of times alarm is set to snooze function, duration of snooze periods, and time of day when alarm is deactivated.

2) Medication adherence: A high percentage of elderly people recently discharged from hospital do not understand the purpose of their medications. Therefore, the increasing number of drugs prescribed at hospital discharge is correlated to low medication adherence or complete non-adherence. It creates a real problem, especially for the elderly person receiving multiple drugs to treat a single condition [9]. This highlights the importance of knowing about medication adherence as well as the elderly person's medication list and regime for caregivers [7]. Caregivers/family members are worried about health problems aggravated by elderly people forgetting to take medication, accidentally taking too much, or even taking someone else's medication. Medication tracking is difficult if the elderly person lives alone. There is no perfect solution to this issue at the moment [10]. Besides accessing adherence statistics and information about medications taken or missed, caregivers/family members will benefit from a refill reminder feature [11].

3) Activity and Physical Exercise: Aging is one of the risk factors of physical and cognitive decline and physical activity is an additional effective non-pharmaceutical measure against aging. The elderly who stay active have reduced risk of such diseases as ischemic heart disease, stroke and diabetes. There is no evidence of physical exercise having a negative impact on cognition [12]. The amount of activity and physical exercise undertaken by the elderly person is of interest to caregivers/family members. For example, they want to know whether the elderly in their care exercise sporadically or on a regular basis. Some caregivers add that it is important for them to know certain metrics of physical ability such as strength and balance [7]. To comprehensively present activity and physical exercise information, such features as activity type, its duration, frequency, and intensity need to be logged.

4) Falls: A fall is an emergency situation and a source of danger to the elderly. Falls are a leading cause of unintentional injury among adults aged 65 and over. Even ground-level falls can result in multiple severe injuries. There are additional dangers if the elderly person lives alone. Most caregivers/family members have to ask the elderly person to carry their mobile phone around the home. The current technology required to detect falls invades the privacy of the elderly person (for example, cameras) while motion sensors may have difficulties detecting falls [8]. A UI fall detection system needs to be able to register an event, correctly identify whether it is a fall, and alert the caregivers/family members if necessary.

5) Localisation: Localisation of the elderly is of high interest to caregivers/family members. They find it important to be aware of the elderly's location in the home and to be notified in case they leave the house unattended to avoid the issue of wandering. Wandering is a very problematic and dangerous type of behaviour of the elderly, which could aggravate possible risks of suffering serious injuries as a result of the disorientation. A series of interviews with family members and with professional caregivers established that both groups of stakeholders prefer to be notified if the elderly person leaves the home for any reason [10]. Despite the fact that a situation where an elderly person leaves the house is not an emergency, compared to a situation where a dangerous fall occurs, it can still lead to hazardous consequences. Additionally, family members, even those who have their elderly relatives living with them in their own homes, expressed an interest in being aware where their elderly relative was in their home at any given point in time. The reasoning behind this is the fact that some areas of the house are not safe (sharp objects in the kitchen, slippery tile floors in the bathroom, etc.) [8]. Thus, information about the elderly's location, duration of stay, and time of entering/leaving the location is essential in a UI.

B. ADL Presentation Methods

ADL data collected from multiple sources over long periods can be a challenge to present efficiently. Which types of presentation convey ADLs in the best way, and how to visualise the relevant information for caregivers/family members, is still relatively unexplored [13]. The goal of using visual displays is to reduce the cognitive load of information and allow users to easily interpret large amounts of data [14]. Modern methods for visually presenting summary statistics include tables, charts, and graphs. They subsequently divide into column, bar, and pie charts, to name but a few. These diagrams are designed to show a considerable amount of information in a concise way, that allows for quick interpretation and understanding [15]. All of these methods could be deployed for presenting ADLs in UIs for caregivers/family members.

Colour carries an important meaning and has an impact on people's cognition and behaviour. Red is implicitly associated with failure and danger [16] and can even undermine performance on challenging tasks that require mental manipulation and flexibility [17]. Yellow is commonly used to indicate caution (e.g., brake lights). Blue and green are associated with positive content and are thought to be experienced as relaxing or cool, encouraging a calm and stable action [18].

Differing fonts have specific emotional and persuasive aspects. In a UI the size and type of font influences its readability. 14-point fonts are found to be more legible, promote faster reading and thus are recommended for presenting online text to users aged 60 years and over. There is no significant difference between the readability of serif (Arial, New Roman) and sans serif (Verdana, Georgia) fonts [19].

Taking into consideration the fact that many caregivers are themselves older [20], a UI must be as easy and user-friendly as possible. Simple ways of delivering ADL information to caregivers/family members are essential.

1) Sleep: Caregivers/family members need to see a detailed sleeping profile which includes the average sleep, sleep efficiency, duration, states and events detected overnight. Additional information such as the number of sleep interruptions, wake-up time, and bedtime can even be switched to another display and different colours for day and night time can be used [21]. Actigraphy is a major assessment tool in sleep research since it can identify changes over time by recording time in bed, total sleep time, sleep efficiency and detect sleep patterns associated with specific sleep disorders [22]. In a UI actigraphy data can be visualised in multiple ways: data plot, velocity plot, acceleration plot, etc., however a typical display includes spikes to signify different activity levels over a horizontal axis which represents a specific time (e.g., 24 hours or a week). These activity levels can be highlighted in different colours, e.g., red to indicate the period when the elderly person is awake, blue to indicate movement while asleep, green as a start of a new event (going to bed or getting out of bed).

2) Medication adherence: An alert as a text message to a mobile phone of a caregiver/family member is a convenient means for informing them of the elderly person's medication adherence or non-adherence [23]. A nonintrusive alternative to a mobile text message is a UI reminder which does not have to be 'pushed', forcing caregivers/family members to interrupt their current activity, since missing a medication is not an emergency situation. Instead the UI can indicate that a reminder can be retrieved and read when it is convenient, so that caregivers/family members will be able to defer follow-up action after receiving such a reminder. Other medication adherence features in a UI, such as adherence statistics viewing and taken/missed medication tracking, can be presented as calendars or timetables with the days highlighted in different colours depending on the type of event. As timetables are used for managing scheduled tasks, it would be possible to check what medication needs to be taken and when it needs to be taken. Highlighting the missed medication in a different colour would allow caregivers/family members to track the adherence statistics. A refill reminder might be another useful feature [11]. It can be visualised as a pop-up text message similar to that of a missed medication.

3) Activity and Physical Exercise: Activity and physical exercise can be presented in several ways in AAL UIs. Traditionally charts, metaphors, and numbers are the most popular techniques to visualise physical activity information [24]. Daily activity can be visualised in the form of a calendar, which interprets the usual patterns of activity as normal, requiring minimal attention from caregivers/family members. If an unusual event occurs, it could be depicted by a different colour (i.e., red instead of green). For example, Tong et al. [25] describe examples of activity and physical exercise visualisation where the data is represented in the form of a clock dial with a circle representing a time span. Each circle represents one month of time and each ring within that circle represents a day. Rings are then divided into 5 minute slots. If the user is active, the slots corresponding to relevant time become brighter in colour. If a caregiver/family member points the mouse over a particular time slot, information on the exact physical activity undertaken, and the time of that activity, is displayed.

4) Falls: The primary UI response to a fall should be an alert to a caregiver/family member. The image-based fall detection system FEARLESS [26] alerts caregivers automatically and the elderly are not required to take any action. The fall detection system developed by Wu et al. [27] sends a fall alarm text which contains fall location URL. By clicking the URL, caregivers/family members will see a map in a web browser where the fall location is tagged. However, a text message might not be enough. A notification in the form of an alarm seems appropriate in this case. There is no doubt that it has to be intrusive and interrupt the current caregiver's/family member's activity, forcing them to take immediate action before returning to whatever they were doing. This alarm has to be actively 'pushed' to a caregiver/family member, rather than simply be made available, so that it is retrieved, or 'pulled', at the recipient's convenience. Moreover, the alarm has to continue until it is manually stopped, which ensures that the caregiver/family member is aware of the fall.

5) Localisation: One needs to distinguish between visualising outdoor and indoor localisation of the elderly. For outdoor localisation, Faria et al. [28] propose a mobile monitoring system for elderly people. Once the location of the elderly person is detected, the UI displays a web page and a caregiver/family member is able to see the corresponding geographical map, where a red asterisk marks the exact location. Indoor positioning should work continuously in real-time and provide the locations of the elderly person in indoor areas [29]. To capture and depict this data, the UI has to be updated on a minute-by-minute basis. One of the options to present visualisation is a line chart with different colour lines representing different locations along the X axis, which is the timeline. Caregivers/family members would be able to see daily patterns and abnormalities within these daily patterns, e.g., if the time spent in bed is unusually long, it will be depicted by a long line in the chart. A pie chart could be an alternative option to visualise the indoor localisation of the elderly. Pie chart slices could represent the different locations of the house, so that caregivers/family members will be aware how much time per day their elderly loved one spends in each room.

III. Comparison and Evaluation of UIs for Caregivers

In this section, the UIs for caregivers of the following AAL systems will be reviewed:

1) HealthKiosk [30],
2) An Intelligent System For Assisting Family Caregivers Of People With Dementia [20],
3) GiraffPlus [31][32],
4) A Home Health Monitoring System Designed To Support Carers In Their Caring Role [33], and
5) A Monitoring System That Provides Feedback Regarding Physical Functioning [34].

Each of these systems is aimed at facilitating the everyday life of the elderly and their caregivers/family members. HealthKiosk is designed by IBM Research in China. It is a family-based healthcare system for health monitoring. It provides continuous monitoring of patients via a user-friendly interface, and can potentially reduce the effort required from care professionals. The Intelligent System For Assisting Family Caregivers Of People With Dementia is designed by Fukuoka University, Japan. It is an easy-to-run and easy-to-maintain system that monitors dementia patients, assessing their activity. It enhances the caregiver's monitoring ability, memory, problem solving and mobility. GiraffPlus is a collaboration between Örebro University, Sweden, Malaga University, Spain, and Lund University, Sweden. It is a telehealth system which supports independent living by the elderly, by addressing a number of issues aiming to enhance their well-being and extend the period of time for which they can live independently. The Home Health Monitoring System is developed by Distance Lab in Forres, Scotland. It allows people to record, track, and share their physiological health, mood, and calendar events. It is intended for use within informal support networks. The Monitoring System That Provides Feedback Regarding Physical Functioning is developed by Maastricht University, the Netherlands, and by the Institute Charles Delaunay at the Université de Technologie de Troyes in France. It provides feedback to elderly people and to their caregivers/family members, regarding the elderly person's physical functioning.

Out of these five AAL systems, only two have been piloted and deployed: HealthKiosk at the Peking University People's Hospital, China and GiraffPlus in real homes in Sweden, Italy and Spain. The remaining three are prototypes in various stages of development.

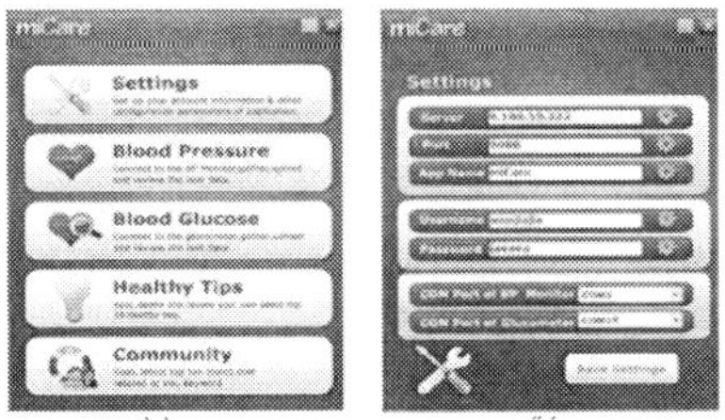

Figure 1. HealthKiosk [30].

In HealthKiosk UI, blue colour is used as a main background (Figure 1). The size of the font is big enough to be convenient to read. It is white against a blue background, and it changes to blue or black if the background is white. On the welcome page, the names of the buttons for different options (settings, blood pressure, blood glucose, community, and healthy tips) are complemented by symbols, e.g., a heart symbol for blood pressure. HealthKiosk offers an easy-to-use UI to interact with the biomedical sensors. The welcome page provides a summary of the functions in a user-centric and service-oriented manner. Users can set their personal settings, take their blood pressure and glucose levels, and browse healthy tips and community suggestions. To view the blood pressure visualisation graphic, the user has to set start and end dates first. Blood pressure is presented as a line graph, with red and blue lines representing systolic and diastolic pressure.

Figure 2. An Intelligent System For Assisting Family Caregivers Of People With Dementia [20].

The web-based UI of the Intelligent System For Assisting Family Caregivers (Figure 2) is minimalistic. When set in the Monitoring mode, it displays a real-time depiction of user's room in the upper left corner of the screen. Clear text on the right states the type of event (e.g., fall) and the place it occurred. The text in the frame shows the pre-scheduled actions. The red bar at the top right displays the level of emergency; the longer the bar, the higher the level of emergency. Below the visual depiction, there are buttons to activate audio communication and to deactivate an alarm. The four buttons at the bottom switch the display window between the Setting, Monitoring and Review operation modes, and access the emergency contacts if necessary. Red or orange text is used for warning or alarm messages, whereas non-alarm messages are shown in green or black. The UI is designed to be easy to understand and to operate.

The Intelligent System For Assisting Family Caregivers provides automatic, unobtrusive 24/7 monitoring, records the elderly person's movement, and it monitors sleep as the sensor network includes a bed sensor. The system allows for medication reminders. It logs the activity of the elderly person, and allows caregivers/family members to view the information for a specified time interval (hour, day, month and year), in the form of graphic or raw data (time, place, activity, generated message). The system is able to detect falls. If a fall occurs, the UI displays a real-time visual of the event on the screen. A text describes the level of emergency and where the event happened. The options for caregivers/family members include activating audio communication with the elderly person, de-activating the alarm, and accessing the emergency contacts if necessary. The system provides monitoring of the elderly person with dementia in their room or flat. Caregivers/family members are able to establish real-time visual and audio communication with the elderly. They can see the frequency or duration of activities such as leaving the room, approaching the entrance door, visiting the toilet, or staying in bed for longer than normal.

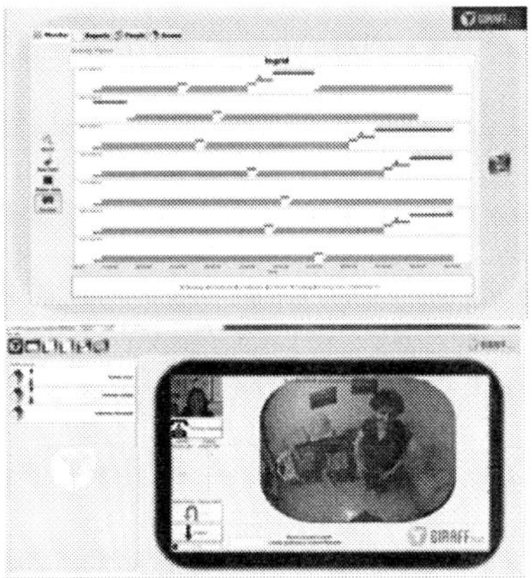

Figure 3. Giraffplus [32].

The UI of Giraffplus (Figure 3) has yellow as its dominating colour and a depiction of a giraffe as its logo. The menu tabs (Monitor, Reports, People, and House) are in the top left corner. The size of the font is quite small; the user would need good eyesight to read the text. The system allows video calls. A Skype-like interface is used: the caller sees the person they are calling, at the same time as seeing themselves on the same screen.

GiraffPlus is able to collect data and analyse long-term patterns in physiological parameters. Sleep and other activities in GiraffPlus are visualised using a line graph, where each activity is represented by different-coloured lines. The green line indicates sleeping, the orange line indicates the elderly person is in the bedroom, the light blue line indicates they are in the bathroom, the light red line indicates they are in the kitchen, the dark red line indicates the elderly person is cooking, the dark blue line indicates they are in the living room, and the yellow line indicates they are watching TV. Giraffplus does not have a medication reminder system, but it is able to present long term data that can show health deterioration. The system does monitor daily activities and the physiological parameters of the elderly person, and it presents a reliable view of their health status for caregivers/family members, as well as for the elderly person themselves. It is also able to detect falls, using its network of home sensors. If an event is recognised as a fall, the alarm is triggered. GiraffPlus detects where the elderly person is, whether he or she is sitting on the couch or lying in bed, using electrical appliances, opening cupboards or the fridge.

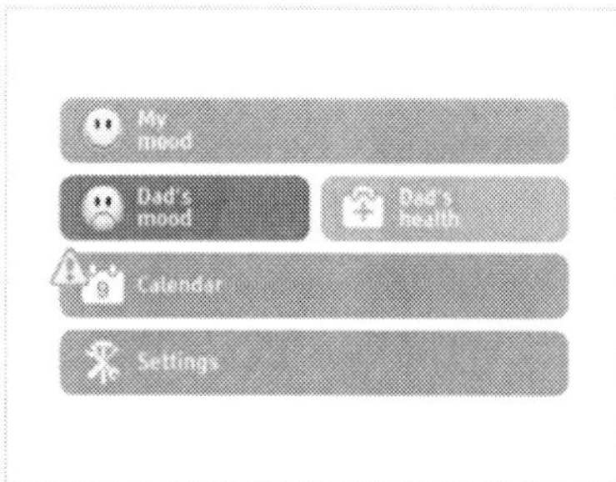

Figure 4. A Home Health Monitoring System Designed To Support Carers In Their Caring Role [33].

The Home Health Monitoring System is created to support family members (Figure 4). The UI consists of several pages; the home page gives an indication of the current mood and health status of the elderly person via an appropriate colour (red, amber, green) and a corresponding smiley face. It is also possible to access the calendar and the settings from the home page. Besides standard traffic-light coding colours, blue and grey are used as neutral colours. The buttons and font are intentionally large to promote quick readability. The system provides a health summary, which lists vital signs, along with the current day's notes. Users are able to enter new readings, view trends (history) graphs, and to compare graphs, which will allow the user to track mood and physiological health over time. The graphs show a week-to-view and plot the average value per day. The system includes a calendar where users can enter events by touching the relevant day. The repeat function can be used for events that happen on a recurring basis such as medication reminders.

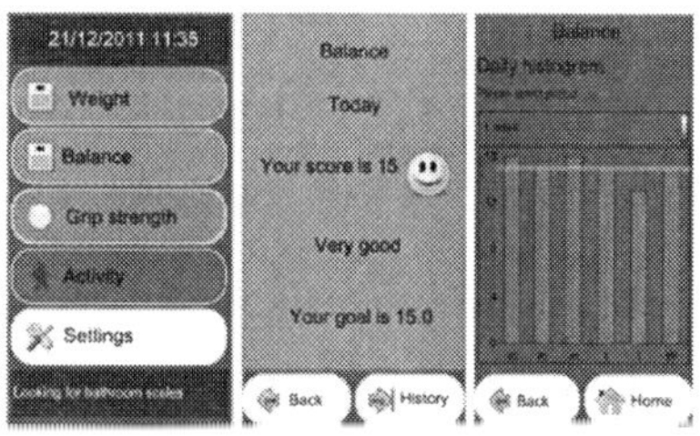

Figure 5. A Monitoring System That Provides Feedback Regarding Physical Functioning [34].

The UI for the Monitoring System That Provides Feedback Regarding Physical Functioning (Figure 5) was designed for a smartphone. The start screen has five large buttons (Weight, Balance, Grip Strength, Activity, and Settings). The text is clearly visible and easy to read. The navigation buttons (Back, History, Home) are clearly marked with appropriate symbols. The background colour of the UI is dark grey, and the buttons are of different colours: green, red, and white.

The UI of the system consists of three layers. The first layer, which is the start screen of the interface, consists of five buttons. When users touch one of the buttons, they enter the second layer, where they receive feedback regarding the measurement they performed. The History button represents the third layer, which provides an overview of the last six balance measurements in the form of a bar chart. The overview time can be set to 2 weeks, 1 month, 3 months, or 6 months, by touching the bar above the graph. When changes are positive, a green background and a smiley face accompany positive feedback messages. If changes are negative, an orange or red background is displayed, combined with an explanatory feedback message.

Out of the five AAL systems, sleep data is presented by the UIs of the Intelligent System For Assisting Family Caregivers, and by Giraffplus. Only the users of the Intelligent System For Assisting Family Caregivers can set reminders for taking medication. Giraffplus, the Intelligent System For Assisting Family Caregivers, and the Monitoring System That Provides Feedback Regarding Physical Functioning track physical activity. Physiological parameters are collected and displayed by the UIs of four systems with the exception of the Intelligent System For Assisting Family Caregivers. Out of these four systems, Healthkiosk, Giraffplus, and the Home Health Monitoring System monitor blood pressure and glucose levels, while the Monitoring System That Provides Feedback Regarding Physical Functioning measures weight, balance, and grip strength. Only the Intelligent System For Assisting Family Caregivers and Giraffplus recognise falls and alarm caregivers/family members. They also track the localisation of the elderly person, moreover, only these two systems are able to establish video communication between the stakeholders.

TABLE I. ADL UI USABILITY ASSESSMENT.

	Sleep	*Medic.*	*Act.*	*Falls*	*Loc.*	*Phys.Data*
HealthKiosk [30]						*X*
Intelligent Sys [20]	*X*	*X*	*X*	*X*	*X*	
GiraffPlus [31] [32]	*X*		*X*	*X*	*X*	*X*
Home Health Sys [33]			*X*			*X*
Monitoring System [34]			*X*			*X*

As can be seen (Table I), each UI of the evaluated systems delivers a set of functions. They coincide to a degree, but hardly include an exhaustive list of features that represents all the needs of caregivers/family members. Yet many people find themselves in a situation where an elderly relative living alone requires more and more attention. This forces the caregiver to look for a compromise, in order to combine their life (which typically includes working and raising children), and caregiving. Usually, personal development, hobbies, and social activities are sacrificed first of all. There exists an obvious demand for a UI which could comprehensively present ADLs, in order to provide a window into the elderly person's daily regime. By remotely visualising ADL information to the caregiver, the UI would provide reassurance that their elderly loved one is functioning normally, thus relieving the caregiver of constant worry about the elderly person's ability to continue living independently.

IV. CONCLUSION

As the world's population inevitably ages, various AAL systems facilitate the independent living of the elderly. They offer support to caregivers/family members, and help alleviate their burden, by presenting some of the elderly person's ADLs in a UI. This paper evaluates a number of UIs in AAL systems in order to compare the main features. The evaluation is based on identified criteria (sleep, medication adherence, activity and physical exercise, falls, localisation) and on the overview of methods that are employed to present ADLs.

It is outlined that the existing UIs meet caregivers'/family members' needs partially. Therefore, for their future work, the authors intend to propose a design of a personalised UI, specifically created to cater for their needs. This UI will be able to track the ADLs of the elderly person, and present them to the caregiver/family member in a simple but meaningful manner, so that they can be reassured that the elderly person is setting about their daily activities.

REFERENCES

[1] D. Monekosso, F. Florez-Revuelta, and P. Remagnino, "Ambient assisted living [guest editors' introduction]," IEEE Intelligent Systems, vol. 30, no. 4. IEEE, 2015, pp. 2–6.

[2] C. Dodd, R. Athauda, and M. T. Adam, "Designing user interfaces for the elderly: A systematic literature review," Australasian Conference on Information Systems, 2017, pp. 1–11.

[3] A. S. Hwang, K. N. Truong, and A. Mihailidis, "Using participatory design to determine the needs of informal caregivers for smart home user interfaces," in Pervasive Computing Technologies for Healthcare (PervasiveHealth), 2012 6th International Conference. IEEE, 2012, pp. 41–48.

[4] M. J. O'Grady, C. Muldoon, M. Dragone, R. Tynan, and G. M. O'Hare, "Towards evolutionary ambient assisted living systems," Journal of Ambient Intelligence and Humanized Computing, vol. 1, no. 1. Springer, 2010, pp. 15–29.

[5] J. Johnson and K. Finn, Designing User Interfaces for an Aging Population: Towards Universal Design. Morgan Kaufmann, 2017.

[6] S. Reinhard, B. Given, N. Petlick, and A. Bemis, "Chapter 14: Supporting family caregivers in providing care," Patient safety and quality: An evidence-based handbook for nurses. Rockville, MD: Agency for Healthcare Research and Quality (US), 2008. http://www. ncbi. nlm. nih. gov/books/NBK2665 [Retrieved: September, 2018].

[7] S. S. Williamson, P. N. Gorman, and H. B. Jimison, "A mobile/web app for long distance caregivers of older adults: functional requirements and design implications from a user centered design process," in AMIA Annual Symposium Proceedings, vol. 2014. American Medical Informatics Association, 2014, p. 1960.

[8] A. L. Zulas, A. S. Crandall, and M. Schmitter-Edgecombe, "Caregiver needs from elder care assistive smart homes: Children of elder adults assessment," in Proceedings of the Human Factors and Ergonomics Society Annual Meeting, vol. 58, no. 1. SAGE Publications Sage CA: Los Angeles, CA, 2014, pp. 634–638.

[9] L. Pasina et al., "Medication non-adherence among elderly patients newly discharged and receiving polypharmacy," Drugs & aging, vol. 31, no. 4. Springer, 2014, pp. 283–289.

[10] A. L. Zulas and A. S. Crandall, "Assessing professional caregiver needs in assistive smart homes," Handbook of Smart Homes, Health Care and Well-Being. Springer, 2017, pp. 121–131.

[11] K. Santo et al., "Mobile phone apps to improve medication adherence: a systematic stepwise process to identify high-quality apps," JMIR mHealth and uHealth, vol. 4, no. 4, 2016, pp. 1–10.

[12] K. F. Felsted, C. Marquez, and D. M. Wischenka, "Benefits of physical activity on cognitive functioning in older adults," Annual Review of Gerontology and Geriatrics, vol. 36, no. 1. Springer, 2016, pp. 103–122.

[13] G. Demiris and H. Thompson, "Smart homes and ambient assisted living applications: from data to knowledge-empowering or overwhelming older adults," IMIA Yearbook, vol. 6, no. 1. Schattauer Publishers, 2011, pp. 51–57.

[14] L. Chittaro, "Visualizing information on mobile devices," Computer, vol. 39, no. 3. IEEE, 2006, pp. 40–45.

[15] K. Potter, H. Hagen, A. Kerren, and P. Dannenmann, "Methods for presenting statistical information: The box plot," Visualization of large and unstructured data sets, vol. 4. Citeseer, 2006, pp. 97–106.

[16] R. Mehta and R. J. Zhu, "Blue or red? exploring the effect of color on cognitive task performances," Science, vol. 323, no. 5918. American Association for the Advancement of Science, 2009, pp. 1226–1229.

[17] A. J. Elliot, M. A. Maier, A. C. Moller, R. Friedman, and J. Meinhardt, "Color and psychological functioning: The effect of red on performance attainment," Journal of experimental psychology: General, vol. 136, no. 1. American Psychological Association, 2007, p. 154.

[18] A. J. Elliot and M. A. Maier, "Color psychology: Effects of perceiving color on psychological functioning in humans," Annual review of psychology, vol. 65. Annual Reviews, 2014, pp. 95–120.

[19] M. Bernard, C. H. Liao, and M. Mills, "The effects of font type and size on the legibility and reading time of online text by older adults," in CHI'01 extended abstracts on Human factors in computing systems. ACM, 2001, pp. 175–176.

[20] V. Moshnyaga et al., "An intelligent system for assisting family caregivers of dementia people," in Computational Intelligence in Healthcare and e-health (CICARE). IEEE, 2014, pp. 85–89.

[21] T. Hao, G. Xing, and G. Zhou, "isleep: unobtrusive sleep quality monitoring using smartphones," in Proceedings of the 11th ACM Conference on Embedded Networked Sensor Systems. ACM, 2013, p. 4.

[22] A. Sadeh, "The role and validity of actigraphy in sleep medicine: an update," Sleep medicine reviews, vol. 15, no. 4. Elsevier, 2011, pp. 259–267.

[23] J. Thakkar et al., "Mobile telephone text messaging for medication adherence in chronic disease: a meta-analysis," JAMA internal medicine, vol. 176, no. 3. American Medical Association, 2016, pp. 340–349.

[24] C. Fan, J. Forlizzi, and A. K. Dey, "A spark of activity: exploring informative art as visualization for physical activity," in Proceedings of the 2012 ACM Conference on Ubiquitous Computing. ACM, 2012, pp. 81–84.

[25] X. Tong, D. Gromala, L. Bartram, F. Rajabiyazdi, and S. Carpendale, "Evaluating the effectiveness of three physical activity visualization-show people perform vs. perceive," IEEE VIS Electronic Proceedings, 2015, pp. 1–4.

[26] H. Weegh and M. Kampbel, "Acceptance criteria of ambient assistant living technologies," Studies of Health Technology and Informatics, vol. 217, 2015, pp. 857–864.

[27] F. Wu, H. Zhao, Y. Zhao, and H. Zhong, "Development of a wearable-sensor-based fall detection system," International journal of telemedicine and applications, vol. 2015, Hindawi Publishing Corp., 2015, p. 2.

[28] S. M. Faria, T. R. Fernandes, and F. S. Perdigoto, "Mobile web server for elderly people monitoring," in Consumer Electronics, 2008. ISCE 2008. IEEE International Symposium on. IEEE, 2008, pp. 1–4.

[29] Z. Wang, Z. Yang, and T. Dong, "A review of wearable technologies for elderly care that can accurately track indoor position, recognize physical activities and monitor vital signs in real time," Sensors, vol. 17, no. 2. Multidisciplinary Digital Publishing Institute, 2017, p. 341.

[30] C. H. Liu, J. Wen, Q. Yu, B. Yang, and W. Wang, "Healthkiosk: A family-based connected healthcare system for long-term monitoring," in Computer Communications Workshops (INFOCOM WKSHPS), 2011 IEEE Conference. IEEE, 2011, pp. 241–246.

[31] S. Coradeschi et al., "Giraffplus: a system for monitoring activities and physiological parameters and promoting social interaction for elderly," in Human-Computer Systems Interaction: Backgrounds and Applications 3. Springer, 2014, pp. 261–271.

[32] S. Coradeschi, A. Cesta et al., "Giraffplus: Combining social interaction and long term monitoring for promoting independent living," in Human system interaction (HSI), 2013 the 6th international conference. IEEE, 2013, pp. 578–585.

[33] A. Taylor, R. Wilson, and S. Agamanolis, "A home health monitoring system designed to support carers in their caring role," in eHealth, Telemedicine, and Social Medicine, 2009. eTELEMED'09. International Conference. IEEE, 2009, pp. 194–199.

[34] J. Vermeulen et al., "User-centered development and testing of a monitoring system that provides feedback regarding physical functioning to elderly people," Patient preference and adherence, vol. 7. Dove Press, 2013, p. 843.